ABIDE
LIVING IN GOD'S PRESENCE

DEBORAH OAKLEY

OAKLEY PUBLICATIONS
Grand Prairie, Texas

Copyright © 2015 by Deborah Oakley

All rights reserved.

ISBN-10: **1505810574**
ISBN-13: **978-1505810578**

DEDICATION

There is only one person that I can rightfully dedicate this book to. He is the only person that was indispensable in the writing and completion of this book. It is with enormous appreciation and heartfelt thanks that I dedicate this book to my brilliant husband Joe Oakley. I will never forget the endless hours you spent teaching me how to write. Your patience equaled that of Job as you edited my manuscript numerous times with a fine tooth comb. I know you bit your tongue many times when I would interrupt the Cowboys game or your favorite show because I needed your help and I needed it now. You never complained when I would ask for help five minutes after you finished your Sunday sermon and just sat down to relax. I must say, you went above and beyond and I could never have written this book without your dedication and help. Of course that is the way it's been our entire marriage. You've always gone out of your way to help me. So I thank you for sacrificially allowing me to interrupt you and for giving up your precious time to help me complete this book. You are my mentor, my example, my encourager and my greatest inspiration. Thank you from the bottom of my heart.

ACKNOWLEDGMENTS

Most of my sources are documented in my book but I also want to acknowledge the use of numerous commentaries, concordances, Sermon Central and *Sparkling Gems: From the Greek Devotional* that influenced my writing. Of course I have also been influenced by countless other authors, preachers and speakers.

CONTENTS

	Dedication	i
	Section One – The Importance Of Abiding In Christ	1
1.	Where Do You Live?	3
2.	Abiding In God's Vineyard	14
3.	Under The Microscope – A Definition Of Abide	23
4.	What Does It Mean To Be In Christ?	33
	Section Two – Three Keys To Abiding In Christ	49
5.	The Presence Of God	51
6.	The Manifest Presence Of God	72
7.	The First Key Is Abiding In Worship	80
8.	The Second Key Is Abiding In God's Word	89
9.	The Third Key Is Abiding In Prayer	95
	Section Three – The Hindrances To Abiding In Christ	113
10.	It's The Little Foxes	115
11.	Call The Horticulturist	131

12.	Press In, Press Out and Press On	136
	Section Four – The Benefits Of Abiding In Christ	147
13.	You Don't Have To Settle	149
14.	The Benefit Of Fruitfulness	155
15.	The Benefit Of Pruning	164
16.	The Benefit Of Love	170
17.	The Benefit Of Freedom	175
18.	The Benefit Of Obedience	182
	Epilogue	191

SECTION ONE

THE IMPORTANCE OF ABIDING IN CHRIST

Abide

-1-
WHERE DO YOU LIVE?

Principles Or Presence?

Learning to abide in God's presence has been a lifelong journey for me. During my first few years as a Christian I had occasional glimpses of God's presence. But, I always yearned for more. I wanted to abide in His presence, not just occasionally experience His presence. God heard the cry of my heart and in 1979 He led my husband and me to Shady Grove Church in Grand Prairie, Texas.

The first time I walked into Shady Grove I knew I was home. It wasn't just because of how friendly the people were or how good the sermon was or how talented the musicians were or the excellent children's ministry. It was because the presence of God was in that place. From the first note on the keyboard to the last word of the sermon... God was there. I could feel Him, sense Him, and hear Him. The atmosphere was charged with the power of the Holy Spirit. People were lifting hands in holy praise. Others were kneeling in brokenness and weeping at the feet of Jesus. Some were bowing in humble acknowledgement that God was in this place. All over the sanctuary God was exalted and glorified through heartfelt praise.

I was home.

For the next ten glorious years God showed up every week. The church grew rapidly. Not just because of following church growth principles, but because of following God's presence.

I remember when my husband would ask our pastor the reason for the growth of the church, he would shake his head, shrug his shoulders and reply, "I don't know. It's just God." The leaders knew all the growth principles, but it was the presence of God that drew people to Shady Grove Church. It wasn't growth principles that changed their lives; it was God's presence that changed their lives.

Principles alone are powerless to transform a heart or heal a hurting soul. Principles alone can't speak to the agony of divorce, abuse, sickness, failure, disappointment, shame, or fear, but God can.

Please understand, I'm not saying that principles aren't important, because I believe they are extremely important. Principles play a major role in providing structure and systems. Principles maintain and facilitate what God is doing and without them the church would not grow. But principles without God's presence are superfluous. It was God's presence that changed my life at Shady Grove Church and His presence can change your life too!

Our season at Shady Grove taught us about God's presence. We practically lived for Sundays so we could get to church. Many times the services were three hours long, but we didn't care. The longer the better because God was there: healing, blessing, saving, touching and changing lives. It was the highlight of our week. We could have pitched a tent and lived there. As you will soon see, that is one of the definitions of the word abide. It means the place where you live. We were living in the presence of God.

So where do you live? I'm not asking if you live in the United States or Texas or California or Florida or any other part of the world. I'm asking where you live your life. Do you live in a place called guilt on Condemnation Cul-de-sac? Do you live in a place called bondage on Sin Street? Do you live on a dead end street called Depression, Discouragement or Despair? Or maybe you live on Rage Road. Or Anger Alley. Or Loser Lane. Or Bitterness Boulevard. Or Pity Parkway.

If you're living in any of these places, it's time for you to have a change of address. You need to move from a place called fear to a place called faith. You need to move from a place called anger to a place called self-control. You need to move from a place called bitterness to a place called forgiveness. And no matter which of these you struggle with, realize that we are all moving to the same place. That place is abiding in Christ.

That's because by definition the word abide means "the place where we live." It means to dwell or to stay in a certain place. Many of us have been living in guilt, condemnation, depression, discouragement, despair, rage, anger, bitterness and more. But we don't have to live like this. We can change our address and not look back. We can have a new life of joy, peace, freedom, abundance, forgiveness, and love. Here's how: by abiding in Christ.

Sounds easy, doesn't it? Just abide in Christ and you'll have love, joy and peace. I don't mean to oversimplify.

Abiding takes perseverance and determination.

It's not a magic formula or a quick fix. You can't just read a book or hear a sermon and voila... you've figured it out. Quite the contrary, abiding is an all-encompassing, all-consuming, all-enveloping relationship with the sovereign presence, our Creator, our Maker, our God and our Lord. It's an unexplainable mystery foreign to our natural mind, an incomparable love story, an unparalleled adventure that will thrill our soul, yet terrify our flesh.

Abiding will call us to live, but require us to die.

Abiding will fill us with hope then sorely test our faith. It's a paradox at best. It will require all we have to give and more. It's not for cowards or the faint of heart. The strong become weak, independence crumbles, pride is crushed into a million pieces. One's life is not their own.

Will You Take The Journey?

Abiding is a free gift of God that will cost us everything. There's no charge for admission, but you can't bring your excess baggage. Whatever weighs you down must be left behind. The journey is long because you never really arrive. It's a journey, not a destination. It's a journey each of us must take if we desire to know God. But it is also the most worthwhile journey all of us will ever take. Here's why.

Jesus is our travel companion. He is always right there with us... in us... before us... behind us... beside us... and even carrying us when necessary. It's a necessary journey because it's the only path that leads to life. It's the path all of us must travel, but unfortunately it's the path less traveled... and that is why I wrote this book.

Consider this book a love letter from your Heavenly Father. He is beckoning you to pack up all your burdens, leave behind all your failed efforts and take the journey to a deeper relationship with the only one who can free your soul. So let's begin our journey of abiding in the presence of God.

The journey is different for each of us, but each of us must take the journey.

In Hebrews 11:8-10 we read about a fellow sojourner. Abraham was a man of faith and it was by faith that he began his journey into the Promised Land. He had no idea where he was going. He just knew he must go and find the place where God dwelt. He was looking forward to the city with foundations, whose architect and builder was God. He wouldn't settle for anything less than the city of God. He was determined to dwell where God dwelt.

So, Abraham made his home in the Promised Land. He lived like a stranger in a foreign country. He slept in tents erected on the cold hard ground: waiting, looking, longing for the time when he would exchange his dusty and worn tent on the ground for a home designed, fashioned and built by the hand of God: a home in a city where God was the architect and builder.

An architect is one who plans, calculates and constructs a building. From start to finish, an architect has his fingerprint on his design. Unlike Abraham, we don't have to go very far to find this building that God designed. 1 Corinthians 3:16 tells us where it is.

Don't you know that you yourselves are God's temple and that God's Spirit lives in you?

We are the place where God dwells. His Spirit lives in us. We don't have to look any farther. God is with us and in us. We have all of God, but the question is: does He have all of us? Or, are we withholding parts of our life from Him? Are there rooms in our house that He can't go into? Have we closed the door and bolted the lock? Does the sign on the door read, "DO NOT

ENTER"? Yes, He abides in us, but we must choose to give Him access to every room in our heart.

Slow Down – Curve Ahead

This doesn't happen overnight. It happens over time... lots of time. Sometimes it feels like time is standing still. Sometimes you feel like you've lost so much time or just lost track of time. But, one thing is for sure: you can't hurry time.

Abiding is learned in the crucible of time.

My initial crucible took ten years. For ten long, painful, and agonizing years I lived in guilt, condemnation, depression, discouragement, disappointment and fear. I would wake up depressed, go to bed afraid and repeat the whole process again the next day. I understood what it meant to abide because I was abiding in hell on earth. I lived in pain. I was imprisoned in fear. I was suffocating spiritually and didn't know how to make it stop.

Satan had so many strongholds in my life that every day was an uphill climb, an obstacle course, a catastrophe. Yes, I was a Christian. A sold out, born again, Bible believing, Spirit-filled child of God. I read my Bible, crawled my way into God's presence, and went to church every time the doors were open. I did it all, but all of it wasn't enough. Something was missing. Something was wrong. Something had to change.

Abide

I needed a change of address and it took me ten years to make that change.

Alright, maybe you think I'm being a little dramatic. I'm really not. I don't want to burden you with too many details, but I think it might make more sense if I tell you my story. Everyone has a story and our stories help us understand each other.

My story goes like this: My mom and dad were separated when my mom was pregnant with me, so the last thing my mother wanted was a baby. We were also poor. So, not only was I unwanted, I was also a financial burden. In order to escape her troubles, my mother marries a man that she thinks will rescue her, but instead he only brings more troubles. He is an alcoholic and a sex addict. I become the object of his sexual obsession. I can't remember how old I was, but I'll never forget the abuse. He drinks before he sexually abuses me. I'm too young to drink so I disassociate to escape the unnatural, disgusting, life-debilitating incidents called sexual abuse.

A child's mind can't comprehend the long term effects of sexual abuse. However, it does explain the long-term recovery and ten years of hell I endured as an adult. Sexual abuse paralyzed me for way too long. It sentenced me to a spiritual prison that took me a decade to escape.

But, I did escape. I escaped when I learned how to abide in Christ. My shackles were broken. My chains were released. My prison doors were opened wide. I packed my bags, grabbed my passport, called the movers, and changed my address forever... and so can you.

Again, I don't want to oversimplify. I'm not saying I never struggle. Of course I do. We all do. But there are big differences between overcoming the daily struggles of life and life-debilitating struggles. Here are the differences: location, duration and debilitation.

First of all, I changed locations. I changed my address. I don't live in a constant place of defeat; I just visit there occasionally. Very occasionally. I used to live there. Now, when I find myself lost and the street sign reads, "Sin Street" or "Pity Parkway" or "Condemnation Cul-de-sac" or "Bitterness Boulevard", I know I've temporarily lost my way. This isn't where I belong. I'm not in a familiar place. This is not my home anymore. I used to live here, but now I don't.

Another difference is duration. Once I've lost my way it doesn't take me very long to get back to where I live. I've traveled this detour, I've encountered this pitfall, and I've been down this road. Once I realize where I am, it doesn't take me long to find my way back.

The last difference is debilitation. In times past my battles with the devil were like a boxing match between me and Mohammad Ali. One punch and I was down for the count. Not anymore. I've toned my spiritual muscles and learned how to dodge Satan's best punches. Even if the enemy wins a round, he isn't going to win the fight. He might knock me down, but I won't stay down. I will rise again and come up fighting. Just like it says in Proverbs 24:16:

For though a righteous man falls seven times, he rises again.

Yes, I've changed my address. My life is characterized by victory, not defeat. I used to live in defeat, now I just visit there on brief occasions. Now I live in Christ, in His word, and in His presence. I'm surrounded by His Spirit. In Him I live and move and have my being. Where He is I am. I feel Him, I hear Him, I recognize His voice when He speaks to me. I know His heartbeat. He is my life, my all in all. I'm never alone. Even when I feel alone, I know I'm not. I know He is with me. He empowers me. He gives me strength. In Him I can do anything. Nothing is too difficult for me when I abide in Him. I know that. Every day I count on Him. Moment by moment I seek His help. He gets me through every second of every minute of every hour of every day... if I abide in Him.

That's what the Bible teaches. We must abide in Christ.

We must live where He lives.
We must dwell in His presence.

Learning to Abide

At the end of each chapter I am including some questions to help you learn how to abide in Christ. This will help you turn information into transformation.

1. Underline which of the following would best describe where you live your life:

   Guilt and condemnation or forgiven?
   Bondage or freedom?
   Depressed or joyful?
   Discouraged or hopeful?
   Rage and anger or self-controlled?
   Feeling like a loser or a winner?
   Worried and anxious or peaceful?
   Hateful or loving?
   Defeated or overcoming?

2. What are some ways you can show God you are determined to abide in Him?

3. What areas of your life are you withholding from God?

-2-
ABIDING IN GOD'S VINEYARD

The Bible refers to our relationship with Christ as abiding. In John 15, John gives an analogy of a vine and its branches. Jesus is the Vine and we are the branches. This is a beautiful word picture from nature that so effectively depicts our relationship with Christ.

The branch is completely dependent on the vine. We are completely dependent on Christ. The branch can do nothing apart from the vine. We can do nothing apart from Christ. The branch cannot bear fruit apart from the vine. We cannot bear fruit apart from Christ. This is the language of John's analogy.

So let's begin our journey by reading the words of Jesus in John 15:1-8:

I am the true vine, and My Father is the vinedresser. Every branch in Me that does not bear fruit He takes away; and every branch that bears fruit He prunes, that it may bear more fruit. You are already clean because of the word which I have spoken to you. Abide in Me, and I in you. As the branch cannot bear fruit of itself, unless it abides in the vine, neither can you, unless you abide in Me. I am the vine, you are the branches. He who abides in Me, and I in Him, bears much fruit; for without Me you can do nothing. If anyone does not abide in Me, he is cast out as a branch and is withered; and they gather them and throw them into the fire, and they are burned. If you abide in Me, and My words abide in you, you will ask what you desire, and it shall be done for you. By this My Father is glorified, that you bear much fruit; so you will be My disciples.

This text is the basis of this book. My prayer is that whatever meaning you derived from these verses is miniscule compared to the revelation you are about to receive from God. I pray He will use every word in this book to deepen your understanding of the most important relationship you will ever have: your relationship of abiding in Christ.

Your spouse, your children, your relatives, your friends, your pastor, your counselor, your boss, your doctor, your accountant... no other relationship on this earth compares to your relationship with God. All other relationships pale in comparison. No one can compete with God. No one cares like God. No one understands you like God.

The above passage gives us the combination to the hidden places of our heart where Christ longs to meet with us. We don't just visit Him on special occasions or times of tragedy; we live with Him. We live in His presence.

Abiding is one word that can thrust you into intimacy with God. One word that can take you from the Holy Place to the Holy of Holies. One

Abide

word that can quench your thirsting soul. One word that can ignite a spark to fan the flame of your smoldering love. One word that can answer the questions that have gone unanswered for so long.

Pack Your Microscope

We are going to dissect John's writing under a microscope until we have a better understanding of what it means to abide in Christ. We will uncover the hidden truths written so long ago by one who followed in the footsteps of Christ.

John knew firsthand what it meant to abide with Jesus. He journeyed with Jesus across the landscape adorned with vineyards. He wrote by divine inspiration that Jesus chose a vine to communicate the truths that define our relationship with Almighty God.

A mystery unfolds as we read the words of John: the only true and righteous God chose to unite Himself with fallen, sinful and depraved man. The almighty King of the Universe, who holds the world in His hands, who defies understanding, who is holy and righteous and just revealed to John - a human vessel - truths that will turn the key, unlock the door, dispel the darkness, and bridge the chasm between fallen man and an all-powerful, all-knowing God.

So let's begin the journey.

You are about to change your address.

You're Moving To A Vineyard

A vine? Why a vine? As we read John 15, I find it compelling that Jesus chose a vine to illustrate our relationship with Him. He could have chosen anything. But He chose a vine.

That's because in Bible days, the vineyard was exceedingly important to the economy and life of Israel. Vineyards adorned the landscape and every Jew understood the relationship between a vine and its branches. They understood that the vine supplied nourishment to all the branches.

So, for Jesus to say that He is the True Vine and we are the branches is saying that Jesus is the source of all nourishment to our souls. He is our life and breath, our power, our strength, our hope, our wisdom, our joy, our peace, our deliverer, our healer, our sustainer, our provider and our all in all. There isn't anything that we are that didn't come from Him. There isn't anything that we have that didn't come from Him. Whether we realize it, acknowledge it or admit it:

Everything we are and everything we have comes from God.

The very breath you just took came from Him. Listen to the words of James as he echoes this truth in James 1:16-17:

Don't be deceived, my dear brothers. Every good and perfect gift is from above, coming down from the Father of the heavenly lights, who does not change like shifting shadows.

This is an important concept if we are to comprehend the vine analogy. We are not our source; Jesus is our source. Our boss is not our source; Jesus is our source. Our spouse is not our source; Jesus is our source. He's the Vine that nourishes us, provides for us and sustains us. Jesus is our Vine.

But He's Not Just A Vine

But notice, John doesn't just say that Jesus is *the vine*. He says Jesus is *the TRUE Vine*. That means there must be false vines or counterfeit vines. Maybe we think money or power or success or things or people will nourish our souls. Those things are counterfeit vines and counterfeit vines will never satisfy our souls.

Counterfeit vines will never bring the fulfillment we long for. Counterfeit vines will never bear good fruit. Only Jesus is the "True" Vine. When we abide in Him – when we live in His presence - we have the fruit of His Spirit: love, joy, peace, patience, kindness, goodness, faithfulness, gentleness, and self-control (Galatians 5:22).

However, there's a condition. IF we abide in Him. John 15:4 says it this way:

Abide in Me, and I in you. As the branch cannot bear fruit of itself, unless it abides in the vine, neither can you, unless you abide in Me.

Nourishment for our souls and bearing fruit in our lives only happens IF we abide in the True Vine.

Consider for a moment every failure you've ever experienced in your life, every mistake you've ever made, and every sinful act that you've ever committed. Without exception, every failure, every mistake and every sin are a consequence of failing to abide in Christ.

You see, it's impossible to sin when you're abiding in Christ. A good tree can't bear bad fruit. You can't do evil when you're encompassed by good. Light and darkness can't exist together. There must be a disconnect for sin to exist. You must cease to abide for sin to appear.

The best recipe for righteous living is to abide in Christ.

Stay connected to the Vine and you will produce good fruit. Unfortunately, we usually do the exact opposite. Instead of abiding we try performing. Our flesh thinks it can please God, so we try to be good by doing good things. But, the flesh can't produce anything good. You could do nothing but good every second of every day for the rest of your life and it wouldn't be good enough to please God. There are many Bible verses that demonstrate the fact that we cannot please God in our own strength. We will never be good enough, strong enough, capable enough or wise enough on our own.

Abide

Romans 8:5-11 says:

For those who live according to the flesh set their minds on the things of the flesh, but those who live according to the Spirit, the things of the Spirit. The mind of sinful man is death, but the mind controlled by the Spirit is life and peace; the sinful mind is hostile to God. It does not submit to God's law, nor can it do so. Those controlled by the sinful nature cannot please God. But you are not in the flesh but in the Spirit, if indeed the Spirit of God dwells in you. Now if anyone does not have the Spirit of Christ, he is not His. And if Christ is in you, the body is dead because of sin, but the Spirit is life because of righteousness. But if the Spirit of Him who raised Jesus from the dead dwells in you, He who raised Christ from the dead will also give life to your mortal bodies through His Spirit who dwells in you.

Jesus Christ is the answer to our sin problem.

We can't conquer sin on our own. We will never win the battle in our own strength. We need God. That's why God is asking us to abide in Him. A simple statement that is anything but simple. That is why we are going to examine this truth in more detail later in the book.

For now, let's focus on what it means to abide. I'm not talking about a watered-down, over-simplified, careless definition of the word. I'm talking about a thorough, in-depth, accurate definition.

I do realize that we will never exhaust the depths of meaning in this word "abide." That's okay. What's more important is that you glean one grain of truth and apply it to your life. One smidgen of truth from God that is applied to your life is worth all the definitions in the world.

So don't get bogged down in all the definitions. I love word meanings so you're about to get a plethora of them. So ask God to quicken your heart and pierce your soul with the truth that will transform your life.

Learning to Abide

1. What things or people do you depend on instead of depending on God?

2. In what areas in your life do you need to recognize Jesus as your source?

3. In what ways are you performing to try to please God?

-3-
UNDER THE MICROSCOPE – A DEFINITION OF ABIDE

In John 15, the Greek word translated "abide" is "meno." It means "to stay in a certain place." The noun is "abode" which means "the place where we live." The King James Version translates abide as: continue, dwell, endure, remain, and stand. Webster's defines it as: "to remain stable." The classical Greek meaning is "to stay and stand fast." So if you put it all together here's the combined definition of abide:

**To stay in a certain place.
The abode where we live.
To continue, dwell, endure, remain, and stand.
To remain stable and to stand fast.**

So how does that apply to our spiritual lives? Where are we supposed to stay, live, or dwell? What are we supposed to endure and how? How do we remain stable and stand fast?

Here's how: we are to be so connected to Jesus - our True Vine - that we live, dwell and make our abode in His presence. We aren't visitors, but permanent residents drawing life from Jesus. And when Satan attacks us, or life is difficult, we endure, remain and stand fast as we draw sustenance from the Vine. We continue in worship, prayer, and the Word and we remain stable and connected to the True Vine. That is what it means to abide.

You Only Have One Mind

As a pastor I have the privilege of getting to know people's personal lives. I get to be there when life is good and when life is difficult. My husband and I are the ones most people will turn to when they want someone to rejoice with them. We are also the ones they will come to when life gets difficult.

Over the years I've come to a sad realization: most people will praise God and serve Him wholeheartedly when everything is going good, but as soon as life gets difficult, as soon as finances get tight or they lose their job or a child rebels or a friend hurts them, then they begin to question God or doubt His Word or quit attending church. As soon as things get tough they stop trusting God and go back to living in doubt and defeat. The Bible calls this being double-minded.

James 1:5-8 says:

If any of you lacks wisdom, he should ask God, who gives generously to all without finding fault, and it will be given to him. But when he asks, he must believe and not doubt, because he who doubts is like a wave of the sea, blown and tossed by the wind. That man should not think he will receive anything from the Lord; he is a double-minded man, unstable in all he does.

By definition, abide means to remain stable. If someone is double-minded they are unstable in every area of their life. It's like having two minds. But, God didn't create us to have two minds. It might feel like we have two minds sometimes. Our thoughts might wander from the truth of the Word, but we don't have to wander very far. God created us to have one mind and that is the mind of Christ. 1 Corinthians 2:16 says:

For who has known the mind of the Lord that he may instruct Him? But we have the mind of Christ.

When you are abiding in Christ, then you have the mind of Christ, you think His thoughts, you have His desires, you feel His feelings, and you want His will. This is the privilege of those who abide. Romans 8:6-9 says:

The mind of sinful man is death, but the mind controlled by the Spirit is life and peace; the sinful mind is hostile to God. It does not submit to God's law, nor can it do so. Those controlled by the sinful nature cannot please God. You, however, are controlled not by the sinful nature but by the Spirit, if the Spirit of God lives in you.

When you abide, your mind is controlled by the Spirit and you have life and peace. If you are controlled by sin you won't submit to God; you can't please God. You are double-minded and unstable. This is what happens when we cease to abide. Being a double-minded, unstable person is a by-product of not abiding. But it doesn't have to be that way because we have the mind of Christ.

It's really easy to identify those who know the place of abiding from those who don't. Watch how people act when trouble comes their way. The ones who fall apart or shake their fist at God are in the "not abiding" category. As soon as trouble comes they abandon their faith until doubt infects their souls like a cancer. They have no stability. They are shipwrecked on the shore of unbelief. They stagger around like drunken men. They're lost and wandering around trying to understand why God failed them. Their address is based on their circumstances, so they constantly move from living in victory to wallowing in defeat. When things are going good – they're up. When things are going bad – they're down. These people are not abiding.

You Are Home To Stay

Wuest's Commentary really explains what I'm trying to say. Wuest defines abide as "a permanence of position, occupying a place as one's dwelling place, and maintaining unbroken communion and fellowship with another." It means to make our spiritual home in Christ: to depend on Him for our spiritual life as the branch is dependent on the vine, to permanently reside in Him. He then supplies us with spiritual energy to produce fruit through the ministry of the Holy Spirit.

This definition leaves no doubt that the tell-tale sign of abiding is maintaining consistent stability in your life.

Stability is proof of abiding.

When you abide, you've come home and you're there to stay. You've unpacked the moving truck, arranged the furniture, made the bed, hung your clothes in the closet, and filled the refrigerator. You've moved in and you're not going anywhere. This is home. This stability is produced by the power of God and sustains us in the good times and the bad. You are abiding in Christ.

Who Flipped The Switch?

Have you ever noticed it's easy to abide when everything is going our way? Like when life is good and God is favoring us, when our prayers are answered, when there's money in the bank, when our spouse listens and agrees with us, when our children obey, when our friends accept us, when our boss appreciates us, and when dreams come true? But, what about the other 364 days of the year?

About three years ago my husband and I were in one of the best seasons of our lives. It was like someone flipped a switch and everything we touched turned to gold. We were on top of the world. Our marriage was awesome. Our health was good. Our finances were blessed. Our children and grandchildren were all behaving.

Abide

Our church was also doing great. Joe and I had just celebrated ten years as pastors of Grace Fellowship Church. We had a "dream team" staff and our church was growing exponentially. And for the first time in eight years I was able to turn over the role of "executive pastor" to one of our staff pastors. This was a long-awaited dream. Then, to top it all off, our church sent us on a trip to Italy to celebrate our twenty-five years in ministry and ten years at Grace Fellowship. Life could not have been better.

It was a season of blessing and favor. Then... someone flipped the switch again. The weekend we arrived home from Italy we received a phone call from one of our pastors letting us know that he was resigning. Now that might not have been such a big deal, but in this instance it felt disastrous. We knew he had to follow what he believed was God's plan for his life. We knew he had to obey the voice of God. We knew our dependency was on God and not a person. However, we still felt like the bottom just dropped out from underneath us.

This particular pastor was our worship pastor AND our executive pastor. He was our right arm. He was THE person we counted on for most things. He was a friend that we loved (and still love). We thought he would be with us forever. Then to top it all off, his wife was our children's pastor. Three key positions and two people who we loved and counted on were leaving. That turned our whole lives upside down.

Looking back I can see that God was showing us that our trust was in Him and not a person. Sometimes God has to pull the rug out from under us to get our attention.

Why am I telling you all this? Here's why: in the years that God poured out His favor on us, I was the poster child for abiding. If you looked up the word abide in the dictionary you would have seen my picture. I was all about being in the Word, praising God, rejoicing, ministering to others and testifying of the goodness of God.

But, all of a sudden, the switch got flipped and it wasn't so easy anymore. Now it was more like, "God, what's going on here? I know You are good, but it sure doesn't feel like it right now. Could we get some help?" It wasn't so easy any more to quote my favorite scriptures or lift my hands in praise or declare the goodness of God. Sometimes all I could do was say, "God help us."

You see, it was easy to "abide" when life was going my way. But, when all hell broke loose, well, that was a different story.

Remember abide means: to continue, dwell, endure, remain, and stand. To remain stable and to stand fast. Listen to the antonyms of abide: decamp, escape, evacuate, get out, abandon, forsake, and vacate.

When times get tough do you escape, evacuate, abandon and forsake worship, the Word and prayer?

Abide

I've had people tell me they haven't been in church because they are going through hard times. I want to say, "WHAT? That's all the more reason to be in church!"

Thayer's Commentary says it like this: to abide means "Something has established itself permanently within my soul, and always exerts its power in me." The moment you begin to doubt, the moment you engage fear or unforgiveness or bitterness or self-pity or any sin is the moment you lose power... it's the moment you cease to abide.

You Light Up My Life

Let me give you an illustration. A missionary in Africa lived in a house that had a generator for electricity. Some locals came to visit him one day. They noticed the light bulb hanging from the ceiling. They were amazed when the missionary flipped the light switch and the light came on. One of the locals asked if he could have one of the bulbs. Not understanding why, the missionary gave him one of the extra bulbs.

Then, one day the missionary visited the man who had asked for the bulb. He led him into his hut and there in the middle of the ceiling was the bulb hanging from a string. Of course there was no light. The missionary had to explain that the light bulb needed electricity to work. It had to be connected to a power source.

The same is true for us. If we want power in our

lives we need to be connected to our power source. Jesus Christ is our power source. Just as electricity provides power for a light bulb to produce light, our True Vine - Jesus - provides power for us – the branches - to produce fruit. However, this only happens if we abide in Him.

Learning to Abide

1. In your own words, what is the definition of abide?

2. On a scale of 1 to 5 (1 meaning hardly ever and 5 meaning most of the time) how often do you abide in Christ?

3. In what ways are you being double minded?

4. The tell-tale sign of abiding is maintaining consistency in your life. In what areas do you need more consistency?

–4–
WHAT DOES IT MEAN TO BE IN CHRIST?

Jesus Christ is our True Vine. So to abide in the Vine means to abide "in Christ." In Christ is where we abide. To "abide in the Vine" and to be "in Christ" are really closely linked. So we need to know what it means to be "in Christ." 2 Corinthians 5:17 says:

Therefore, if anyone is in Christ, he is a new creation; the old has gone, the new has come!

You're Not The Same Person You Used To Be

When we invited Jesus into our lives, we became a new creation "in Christ." The person we used to be is gone! We are a new person in Christ. The Bible calls it the old man and the new man. The old man is the person we were before we were born again. That person is dead and we are a new creation "in Christ."

To be "in something" is to be surrounded by and contained by it. For instance, when you put a letter in an envelope – wherever the envelope goes, the letter goes. Or, when you are in a car you are contained by that car. Wherever it goes you go. If it stops you stop. If it turns you turn. A good example is an unborn baby within its mother. Wherever the mother goes, the baby goes. What the mother does, the baby does. What the mother eats, the baby eats.

We are in Christ: we died with Him, we are buried with Him and resurrected with Him. We abide in Him and He abides in us. We are surrounded by Him. We live in His presence. Where He goes we go. His thoughts are our thoughts. His strength is our strength. His righteousness is our righteousness.

1 Corinthians 1:30 says:

You are in Christ Jesus, Who has become for us wisdom from God - that is, our righteousness, holiness and redemption.

This is who we are in Christ. We changed from being lost in sin to being righteous in Christ. We have a new divine nature. 2 Peter 1:4 says that:

He has given us His very great and precious promises, so that through them you may participate in the divine nature and escape the corruption in the world caused by evil desires.

Our old nature was to sin and please ourselves. Our new nature is to please God.

Our old nature was to do things our way, to exert our will, to live for ourselves. Our new nature is to do God's will, to lose our life, and to live for Him. Christ's divine nature now permeates our being, transforms our lives, renews our minds, and cleanses our hearts. His power flows through us, His grace enables us, His love sustains us, and His mercy upholds us.

This quote by Hannah Whitall Smith exemplifies what I'm saying. "Once it was "I and not Christ." Next it was "I and Christ." Perhaps now it is "Christ and I." But it has yet to come to be "Christ only and not I at all." If there are two wills, two interests, two lives, you have not lost your life. You have not surrendered your will."

Now that does not mean we never sin. There will always be a struggle between spirit and flesh, but we don't have two natures, one good and one bad. It's important that we understand this. We have the nature of Christ after we are born again. Nature means the essence of something – what it is at its core. A bird's nature is to fly. A fish's nature is to swim. A sinner's nature is to sin and please self. A saint's nature is to live holy and please God. Romans 6:6-7 says:

For we know that our old self was crucified with Him so that the body of sin might be done away with, that we should no longer be slaves to sin— because anyone who has died has been freed from sin.

When you were saved your tendency to sin changed. It was nailed to the cross. It's dead. So if you are dead to sin... sin cannot affect or influence you. It has no power over you. The old you – the one that wanted to sin - died and a new you was born.

Colossians 3:3 says you died and your life is now hidden with Christ in God. Ezekiel 36:26 says you have a new heart and a new spirit. I Corinthians 2:16 says you have the mind of Christ. 2 Corinthians 5:21 says:

God made Him who had no sin to be sin for us, so that in Him we might become the righteousness of God.

You are righteous. You may not feel righteous, but you are. When God looks at you He sees His righteousness.

Someone once asked Michelangelo how he created such magnificent sculptures. He answered, "I see something inside the stone, like an angel or a person, and I cut away everything that's not them until all that's left is them." That's what God does in us. He sees who we are in Christ and He cuts away everything that's not really us until all that's left is who we are in Christ.

The Christian life is simply becoming who you are in Christ.

But many times there is a huge discrepancy between how God sees us and how we see ourselves. He sees us "in Christ." We sce ourselves "in the flesh." He sees us as His righteousness. We see us ourselves as ungodly sinners. He sees us as justified and forgiven. We see ourselves as condemned and bound by our mistakes. He sees us as more than conquerors. We see ourselves as failures. He sees us as fearfully and wonderfully made. We see ourselves as ugly, fat, and unacceptable.

You Are Your Own Worst Critic

An experiment was done by The Dove Company with a group of women as the participants. A criminal sketch artist did a sketch of each woman. However, instead of looking at them, he sketched them based on their description of themselves. Then he did a second sketch of the same women. This sketch was based on the description of someone who just met them for the first time.

The first sketch which was based on the women's self-description was consistently less attractive than the women actually appeared. The second sketch, which was based on the description of someone they just met, was in every case much more realistic and attractive.

The discrepancy in how these women saw themselves and how a total stranger saw them is like the difference between how God sees us and how we see ourselves. We see every flaw and every imperfection. God sees a work of art... His work of art. God sees His magnificent and beautiful creation. Psalms 139:13-14 says:

For You created my inmost being; You knit me together in my mother's womb. I praise You because I am fearfully and wonderfully made: Your works are wonderful, I know that full well.

Abide

We are wonderfully made. So why are we so hard on ourselves? Why are we so critical about our looks? We criticize our hair color, our eye color, our skin color, our body shape. We beat ourselves up and put ourselves down because we don't like the way we look. Yet, if God's works are wonderful, then who are we to criticize what God made? Besides, our bodies are the temple of God. He abides in us and He loves us just the way we are. Galatians 2:20 says:

I have been crucified with Christ and I no longer live, but Christ lives in me.

You see:

I am a child of God through faith in Jesus. (Galatians 3:26)
I am redeemed by Jesus' blood and my sins are forgiven. (Ephesians 1:7)
I am a citizen of heaven. (Philippians 3:20)
I am predestined to be conformed to the image of Christ. (Romans 8:29)
I am being renewed inwardly day by day. (2 Corinthians 4:16)
I am His sheep, I hear His voice and I follow Him. (John 10:4)
I have a spirit of power, of love and of self-discipline. (2 Timothy 1:7)
I submit myself to God. I resist the devil, and he must flee from me. (James 4:7)
In all things I have complete victory in Jesus who loves me. (Romans 8:37)
I have every spiritual blessing in Jesus. (Ephesians 1:3)

Do you know who you are "In Christ?" Do you find your true identity in Him?

Open Mouth - Insert Foot

It was at a conference on co-dependency that I realized I was not finding my identity in Christ. Instead my identity was in my husband. I was a classic textbook case of a co-dependent: someone who doesn't know who they are and who derives their sense of worth from another person.

After the conference I mustered up the courage to talk to the speaker. I thanked him for helping me realize how co-dependent I was. That's when he asked me a question. A question that I will never forget: "WHAT DO YOU DO?" Suddenly I heard my mouth saying, "MY HUSBAND IS A PASTOR."

I'll never forget the look on his face. It was a look that said, "What did she just say?" I could almost hear his thoughts, "Did I just ask this woman what she does and she answered 'My husband is a pastor'?" "No," he responded, "the question was what do you do? NOT what does your husband do?"

All I remember next was babbling some lame answer and getting out of there as fast as I could. That day I realized I didn't know who I was in Christ. So let me ask you: Do you know who you are in Christ? Or is your identity in someone or something else?

Roll Out The Red Carpet

For example, do you know that you are royalty? 1 Peter 2:9 says:

But you are a chosen generation, a royal priesthood, a holy nation, His own special people.

We are royalty! What does it take to be royalty? You must be the king or a member of the king's family. The king may have fought his whole life to have obtained his kingdom, but what did his children have to do to attain royalty? Be born! God is the great King. Jesus is the King of kings.

We are children of the King.
That makes us royalty.

We are heirs of the King, we have the rank of a king, we have the rights of a king, and we have the power and authority of a king. We are royalty because our heavenly Father is the King of Kings and Lord of Lords! It's not because we are so great, it's because we are in Christ.

Revelation 5:10 says God made us *...to be a kingdom and priests to serve our God, and they will reign on the earth.* That's who we are: the redeemed, the blood-bought church, kings and priests, holy and set apart by God.

Another way of saying this is that we are saints. Most people have the wrong view of what a saint is. They believe that a saint is a dead holy person officially recognized by the church, or a really, really virtuous person. It's like when people talk about their grandmother, "She was such a saint." However, the Bible teaches that when we accept Christ as Lord and Savior, we are made righteous; we are made saints.

Sainthood is not attained by really holy people who do really righteous acts. God says if you are a Christian, you are a saint. 1 Corinthians 1:2 says:

To the church of God which is at Corinth, to those who are sanctified in Christ Jesus, called to be saints, with all who in every place call on the name of Jesus Christ our Lord.

All people who call Jesus their Lord are saints.

Being saints doesn't mean we are perfect, but it means we are righteous. We are right with God. Why? Because we are in Christ. We are His righteousness. We no longer have to live under the weight of condemnation and guilt. We don't have to go around feeling like we're never good enough.

I'll never forget the time in my life when God began to reveal this to me. Up until this point I had lived under so much condemnation that I never felt like I was good enough. I wasn't a good enough Christian. I wasn't a good enough wife. I wasn't a good enough mother. I wasn't a good enough friend.

Abide

When I was a child my step father would constantly tell me things like, "You don't have a brain in your head" or "You'll never amount to anything." And I believed him. So I grew up feeling stupid, worthless, and ashamed on the inside. I didn't think I could ever amount to anything in life and I certainly didn't believe I was righteous.

Then one day, when I was feeling really down on myself, I heard God say to me: "Every time you put yourself down and every time you condemn yourself it's like a slap in My face." God went on to tell me how every time I beat myself up I was making His sacrifice on the cross null and void in my life and that was like a slap in His face. I heard Him say to me, "I died so that you could be justified, so that you could be righteous, forgiven, cleansed, and set free. Every time you punish yourself you are rejecting My gift on the cross. You're choosing to believe what you say about yourself instead of what I say about you. You're choosing to believe what others say about you instead of what I say about you. You're choosing to believe what Satan says about you instead of what I say about you."

From that day on I have never been the same. That revelation started a reformation in my life. I saw for the first time who I was in Christ. The question is: do you know who you are in Christ? Do you know that you are no longer in darkness? You now walk in light. You once had no mercy, but now you have obtained mercy. You once were blind, but now you see. You once were condemned, but now you are pardoned. You were once lost in your sin, but now you are the righteousness of God.

Let me ask you a question that will help you understand just how righteous you are in Christ. On a scale of 1-10 – 1 being totally unrighteous and 10 being righteous, how righteous is Christ? The correct answer is 10. On a scale of 1-10 – 1 being totally unrighteous and 10 being righteous, how righteous are you? If you are an unbeliever the only correct answer is 0. You have no righteousness apart from Christ. But, if you are a believer in Christ Jesus, the only correct answer is 10 because now you have received Christ's righteousness, which is a 10. It is very important to understand this.

Most Christians say they are just sinners saved by grace. There is truth to that, but we must move past seeing our basic identity as sinners and start seeing ourselves as we are now: saints. If we see ourselves as sinners we will sin. Proverbs 23:7 says:

For as he (a person) *thinks within himself, so he is.*

If you see yourself as a loser, you'll lose. If you see yourself as a winner, you'll win. If you see yourself as a failure, you'll fail. If you see yourself as a sinner, you'll sin. If you see yourself as righteous, you'll live righteously. If you see yourself as royalty, you'll reign.

Abide

You will always produce around you what you cultivate within you.

How you see yourself on the inside will greatly impact what you do on the outside because what you see is what you get. Which raises a really pertinent question: how many opportunities have you missed because you didn't see yourself as an heir of God? You see, what you do is determined by who you think you are.

Tara Holland had a dream to be Miss America. In 1994, she entered the Miss Florida pageant and only won the title of first runner up. In 1995, she tried again and still only won first runner up. Tara was tempted to give up, but in 1997 she won the title Miss Kansas. That same year she was crowned Miss America. Tara Holland saw her dream come true.

During an interview, someone asked Tara the secret to her success. She admitted she was tempted to give up, but instead she went out and rented dozens of videos of local pageants, state pageants, Miss Teen, Miss Universe, Miss World, and whatever she could get her hands on.

She would sit and watch them over and over. As each woman was crowned a winner, Tara would she herself being crowned a winner. She pictured herself walking down the runway in victory. Over and over she saw herself as a winner. This is what Tara said was the key to her success.

When a reporter asked her if she was nervous, Tara's response was, "No, I wasn't nervous at all. You see, I had walked down that runway thousands of times before." I ask you today, have you ever walked down that runway? Are you accomplishing your dreams? Remember, you will become what you think yourself to be.

We are royalty, we are saints and we are also heirs. Colossians 1:12 says:

Giving thanks to the Father, who has qualified you to share in the inheritance of the saints...

An heir is someone who receives an inheritance. An inheritance is not earned – it is given. As children of God, we have an inheritance. John 10:10 says:

The thief comes only to steal and kill and destroy; I have come that they may have life, and have it to the full.

This means we inherit an abundant life of blessing right now. You're more than just a sinner saved by grace; you're royalty, you're a saint, you're an heir of Christ. Don't live beneath your position in Christ!

If you've been living at a dead end street called Depression, Discouragement or Despair... If you're living on Rage Road, or Anger Alley, or Loser Lane, or Bitterness Boulevard, or Condemnation Cul-de-sac, or Pity Parkway, right now you can turn in a change of address.

Abide

Don't let Satan keep you bound to your past. When Satan reminds me of my past, I remind him of his future. With three spikes and a cross Jesus conquered the devil and disarmed him of all power over me forever. With His blood Jesus cleansed me of my past and set me free. Today, you too can be free.

Learning to Abide

1. Describe how you see yourself in Christ.

2. On a scale of 1 – 10 how righteous are you?

3. List some ways you are hard on yourself.

4. What would you do differently if you understood your position in Christ?

5. Are there any opportunities or dreams you have missed due to a misconception of who you are in Christ?

6. What steps of action do you need to take to pursue your dreams?

Abide

SECTION TWO

THREE KEYS TO ABIDING IN CHRIST

Abide

−5−

THE PRESENCE OF GOD

A Small Piece Of Metal With Great Significance

When my parents gave me a key to our house I knew instinctively that this was a right-of-passage. I was no longer an untrustworthy child; I was morphing into a mature, capable teenager who was worthy to carry the key to the house. A small piece of metal had redefined my self-image, bolstered my confidence and empowered me with a new authority. It was a big deal.

Unfortunately, I didn't always prove worthy of this new-found trust, but having that key gave me a new-found freedom. I now could come and go as I pleased. I didn't have to knock on the door when I returned home. All I had to do was insert the key into the keyhole and the door would open.

Keys are a big deal in the Bible. In Matthew 16:19 Jesus said:

I will give you the keys of the kingdom of heaven; whatever you bind on earth will be bound in heaven, and whatever you loose on earth will be loosed in heaven.

This passage tells us that the keys of the kingdom of heaven are connected to our ability to bind and loose. That's a staggering thought.

The power and authority to bind and loose are represented by a set of keys.

Think about the keys on your key ring. Each key gives you access to something. For example, most of us have car keys, house keys, work keys, and keys to our mail box. Without these keys we wouldn't be able to drive, get into our house, do our job or get our mail. A lot depends on keys.

It wouldn't be an exaggeration to say that keys represent power, authority, freedom, and accessibility. It also wouldn't be an assumption to say that keys are helpful when attempting to unlock the treasure chest of God's Word. Understanding how to abide in Christ is like a bolted treasure chest... and God has given us the keys to that treasure chest in His Word.

If you seriously want to learn to abide you must use these keys. Maybe that explains why so many Christians never learn to abide: they're trying to open the treasure chest without the key. Their intentions are good, but their method is misguided.

If you really want to abide in Christ you must use the keys God gave you to succeed.

In John 15:7, Jesus gives us three keys to abiding.

If you abide in Me, and My words abide in you, you will ask what you desire, and it shall be done for you.

So let me break this down for you:

"If you abide in Me..."
The first key is abiding in worship.

"...and My words abide in you..."
The second key is abiding in the Word.

"...ask what you desire..."
The third key is abiding in prayer.

No Magic Wand

Worship, the Word and prayer are the three keys to abiding in Christ.

These three keys tell us what to do and they show us how. That means we don't just come to church and worship if we feel like it; we make church attendance a priority. That means we don't just read the Word when it's convenient; we make reading the Word a priority. That means we don't just pray when we're in trouble or when we want something from God; we make prayer a daily priority.

Now don't get overwhelmed. I can almost read your mind: "I've tried all this before and I failed." Remember, it's not your power but His power that is working in you. Zechariah 4:6 says:

'Not by might nor by power, but by My Spirit,' says the Lord Almighty.

You may have failed a thousand times before, but that's okay. This time is different. This time you won't fail. This time you're going to depend on the Spirit of God to empower you. If you want to know God in a deeper way, if you want to understand the riches of His glory, if you want to abide... you must do it God's way.

Maybe you were hoping for a magic formula. Well, there is no magic formula. There never will be a magic formula. But that's okay because God's ways are higher than our ways. And it's going to be so worth it. Your life is about to change forever. You are about to embark on the greatest adventure of your life. And you'll need three keys... three small pieces of metal to begin your adventure... but not just yet.

First Things First

Before I elaborate on the three keys to abiding in God's presence I want to talk about the presence of God.

> **The presence of God is what abiding is all about. Without God's presence, abiding is unnecessary.**

If you don't understand His presence you could miss the entire purpose of abiding. For example, you could worship every day, pray religiously, and wear out the pages of your Bible from reading. But, unless you understand God's presence, you are not abiding. If you don't have a real, honest-to-goodness relationship with God, then you are just spinning your wheels. It's all about knowing God and having a relationship with Him.

Moses is a really good example of what I'm talking about. In Exodus 33:1-17 God spoke to Moses and told him to lead the Children of Israel to the Promised Land. That was good news because that's what Moses had wanted to do since he led God's people out of Egypt.

The Promised Land was a land flowing with milk and honey and with grapes the size of a man's hand. I imagine Moses was ready and willing to obey. Then on top of the good news was more good news: God promised to send an angel before Moses to drive out all their enemies. I would guess Moses was packing his bags, watering his donkeys, pulling up his tent stakes and preparing for this long awaited journey... nothing could stop them now.

Wrong. There is one thing that did stop them; one thing that was a deal breaker; one thing that changed everything. That one thing was the most important thing that Moses cared about and the only thing that could stop him in his tracks. That one thing wasn't the evil King Pharaoh; it wasn't fear of their enemies or lack of provision or a change of mind. That one thing was God's presence. God wasn't going with them.

God told Moses the people were a stiff-necked people and He wasn't going with them because He might end up destroying them on the way. The one and only thing that could keep Moses from God's promise was if God wasn't going with him.

So what does Moses do? He does what he always does. He goes to the Tent of Meeting to pray. Why? Because going without God wasn't an option for Moses. The Bible says Moses would speak to God face to face as a man speaks to his friend. Moses was a friend of God. He knew God by name. Going without God wasn't a choice for him. Exodus 33:12-17 records Moses' conversation with God.

Moses said to the Lord, "You have been telling me, 'Lead these people,' but You have not let me know whom You will send with me. You have said, 'I know you by name and you have found favor with me.' If You are pleased with me, teach me Your ways so I may know You and continue to find favor with You. Remember that this nation is Your people." The Lord replied, "My Presence will go with you, and I will give you rest. Then Moses said to Him, "If Your Presence does not go with us, do not send us up from here. How will anyone know that You are pleased with me and with Your people unless You go with us? What else will distinguish me and Your people from all the other people on the face of the earth?" And the Lord said to Moses, "I will do the very thing you have asked, because I am pleased with you and I know you by name."

Moses understood that the presence of God was worth giving up everything else. His relationship with God meant more to him than anything.

Presence Versus Promise Versus Presumption

Moses was supposed to lead the Children of Israel into their Promised Land, but he was willing to give up the Promised Land for God's presence. God's presence meant more to Moses than God's promises. Moses wasn't promise-driven; he was "presence-driven." Living without God's presence wasn't an option to Moses. And it shouldn't be an option to us either.

Abiding in God's presence means that everything we do, everything we say, everything we experience and everywhere we go or don't go is DRIVEN by following God's presence.

Moses refused to take one step without the presence of God. He learned this early in his life. He had a call from God to lead the people of God, but at first he tried to fulfill that call in his own way in his own strength in his own time.

He ended up killing an Egyptian and having to run for his life. He ended up spending forty years on the backside of a desert! He learned how much he needed the presence of God by seeing the results of not having the presence of God! That changed him. Moses didn't want to go anywhere or do anything unless the presence of God was with him.

What about you? Are there places you want to go in life? Are there things you really want, like a new job or getting married or moving to a new place or buying a house or taking your dream vacation? Moses said to God, "If Your presence doesn't go with us, don't send us up from here." Can you say the same?

You see, the Children of Israel had a choice. They could go without God. They had that choice and so do we. We can go without God, but not without paying a price. We can make our own decisions about where we live, who we marry, what job we choose, what church we attend, how we spend our money, if we tithe or not, if we go to church or not, if we pray, read our Bible, or if we accept Jesus as our Lord and Savior.

But we will not succeed if we go without God! We will not be blessed if we go without God. We will not be fulfilled if we go without God. We can go without God, but the result is defeat. We can go without God, but the result is devastation. We can go without God, but the result is death... death to our dreams, our blessings, our families, our marriages, our health, and our lives.

This is what happened to the Children of Israel in Numbers 14:40–45. They disobeyed God and then tried to fight an enemy without God.

"We will go up to the place the Lord promised." But Moses said, "Why are you disobeying the Lord's command? This will not succeed! Do not go

up, because the Lord is not with you. You will be defeated by your enemies.... Because you have turned away from the Lord, He will not be with you and you will fall by the sword."
Nevertheless, in their presumption they went up toward the high hill country, though neither Moses nor the ark of the Lord's covenant moved from the camp. Then the Amalekites and Canaanites who lived in that hill country came down and attacked them and beat them down all the way to Hormah.

In presumption the Children of Israel sought God's promises without God's presence and it resulted in defeat at the hands of their enemies.

Presumption is putting confidence in anything other than God. It's when:

- We base success on our abilities, our education or our talents.
- We look for contentment in distractions or busyness.
- We look for love in all the wrong places.
- We look for solace at the bottom of a bottle.
- We look for escape in entertainment.
- We try to fill the God-shaped vacuum within us with anything but God.

Deep inside our soul is longing for the presence of God. When we are presence-driven we can stand when everything seems to be falling apart. We have peace in the chaos of life. We can love when we want to hate. We accelerate all that God has for us because we seek His presence.

Abide

We can experience the uninterrupted presence of God in our lives every day all day.

24/7

The presence of God is always with us, but we are not always aware of it. However, when we abide, we are aware that God is always with us. When we are in prayer we know He is near, our prayers are God inspired, our hearts are overflowing with peace and gratefulness, our burdens are lifted, and our faith lifts us above all worry and fears. When we are at work we know He is near, He is working beside us, problems get solved, finances come through, we have favor with all the right people, doors of opportunity open and we know only God could make it happen.

We know God is near when we are blessed, when we are hurting, when we are happy, when we are sick, uncertain, lost, confused or afraid.

Whenever, wherever, and whatever... God is always near!

You see, there doesn't have to be a distinction between a time of work and a time of worship. We can experience God in all things and feel His presence whether we are at work or at play. We think of God all the time, whether it's day, or night. Whether we're praying or exercising or shopping or watching TV, He is always near.

When we don't feel God's presence, we cry out to

Him. When He draws us, we run after Him. We learn to grow in God's presence little by little, step by step. We stop making prayer a duty and just seek to be in His presence.

Now you may already have a good relationship with God and an extensive understanding of what it means to live in His presence... and that's good. For you this may be a refresher course. For others it may be an introduction to a new way of life. Maybe you don't know God at all. If that's the case you can ask Jesus into your heart right now by praying the following prayer:

"Dear God, I come to you in the name of Jesus. I admit to You that I am a sinner and I need You to save me. I repent of my sins and I need Your forgiveness. I believe that You sent Your Son, Jesus Christ, to die on the cross and to shed His blood for my sins. I ask you to save me by the blood of Jesus and to cleanse me from all my sin. You said in Romans 10:9 that if we confess with our mouth that "Jesus is Lord," and believe in our heart that God raised him from the dead, we will be saved. Right now I confess Jesus as the Lord of my life. With my heart, I believe that God raised Jesus from the dead. I accept Jesus Christ as my Lord and Savior and according to His Word, right now I am saved. Thank you Jesus for Your grace which has saved me from my sins. Thank you Jesus for dying for me and giving me eternal life."

If you sincerely prayed this prayer then you can

celebrate that today is the day of your salvation. Whether you just prayed this prayer for the first time or you've known God your whole life, the goal is to know Him more... and this is why we abide. The purpose is to know God, experience God, and have relationship with God in a deeper and more meaningful way.

So let me ask you a question: do you know that God is with you all the time? He never leaves you. Wherever you go He goes too. You can't escape from God. Theologians call this the omnipresence of God. It means God is everywhere at one time and at all times.

According to the *Encarta Dictionary* it means: He is continuously and simultaneously present throughout the whole creation. But, just because God is there doesn't mean you acknowledge that He's there or that you have a relationship with Him. Just because God is present doesn't mean you are "in" His presence. He could be right there and you're not even aware of it. In Genesis 28:16 Jacob said:

Surely the Lord is in this place, and I was not aware of it.

Why Me God?

One of my favorite authors is A.W. Tozer. In his book *The Pursuit of God* he eloquently puts into words what I'm trying to say: "Why do some persons "find" God in a way that others do not? Why does God manifest His presence to some and let multitudes of others struggle along in the half-light of imperfect Christian experience?"

"The difference lies not with God but with us. Pick at random a score of great saints whose lives and testimonies are widely known. You will be struck instantly with the fact that the saints were not alike. How different, for example, was Moses from Isaiah; how different was Elijah from David."

"I venture to suggest that the one vital quality which they had in common was spiritual receptivity. Something in them was open to heaven, something which urged them Godward... they had spiritual awareness and that they went on to cultivate it until it became the biggest thing in their lives. They differed from the average person in that when they felt the inward longing they *did something about it*. They acquired the lifelong habit of spiritual response."

The point here is that God is always with you, but if you want to know Him you must respond to His presence. The truth is that you are as close to God as you want to be.

You determine your depth of relationship with God by your response to Him. He won't force Himself on you. You get to choose.

**We make our choices and then
our choices make us.**

Abide

The apostle Paul chose to make knowing God his one aspiration and he became the author of two-thirds of the New Testament. David chose to seek God and became known as a man after God's own heart. His response to God is recorded in Psalm 27:4:

One thing I ask of the Lord, this is what I seek: that I may dwell in the house of the Lord all the days of my life, to gaze upon the beauty of the Lord and to seek Him in His temple.

In the Hebrew language the word "seek" means "to search and to strive after." The King James translates it: "to ask, beg, desire, and enquire." David sought one thing – the presence of God – and it resulted in him being a man after God's heart.

Abraham is another good example. When God called Abraham to leave his homeland and follow Him, three things happened. These three steps are necessary if we want to know God. They are: Initiative, Response and Results.

The first step is that God took the initiative. Genesis 12:1 says:

The LORD had said to Abram, Leave your country, your people and your father's household and go to the land I will show you.

God initiated by speaking to Abram and telling him to leave his country. One of the main ways

God initiates in our lives is by speaking to us. John 10:27 says:

My sheep hear My voice, I know them, and they follow Me.

In this passage, God initiated by speaking and the expectation is that we respond by following.

Again, in Song of Solomon 1:4 we see God initiating and the prospect of us responding.

Draw me away! We will run after You.

According to Strong's Concordance the meaning of the word "draw" is very thought provoking. It means "to sow." The implication is that God sows His Word in our hearts. It also means "to sound." The implication here is that God is speaking His Word to our hearts.

So we can conclude that God draws us and God initiates by sowing His Word in our hearts and speaking His Word to our hearts. So this verse could read: Sow your Word in my heart and speak your Word to my heart and I will run after you.

God takes the initiative by speaking His Word to us and by sowing His Word in our hearts. Our part is to respond. You see God is always the initiator. Theologians call this "prevenient grace" which, according to A.W. Tozer, means that "before a man can seek God, God must first seek the man." Our pursuit of Him is dependent on His pursuit of us.

Our hunger and thirst for God comes from God. Even our desire for Him comes from Him. A.W. Tozer also says:

"The impulse to pursue God originates with God. All the time we are pursuing Him we are already in His hand. Our search for Him is responding to His already having found us."

God initiates and we respond. And God always takes the initiative, especially when He is about to accomplish His purposes in our life. And that leads us to the second step to knowing God: Abram responded to God's initiative. Genesis 12:4 says:

So Abram left, as the LORD *had told him.*

Sometimes we're waiting for God to move and God is saying, "It's your move."

When God reveals His heart to us - when He speaks to us, when He sows His Word in our heart, when He draws us - we have a choice: to respond or not to respond.

This is one of the most crucial moments in knowing God. This is where so many fail: because they don't respond. Then, they wonder why they can't hear God, or why they can't find God's will for their lives, or why they aren't being blessed. Blessing follows obedience.

Psalm 27:8 says:

When You said, "Seek My face," My heart said to You, "Your face, LORD, I will seek."

Nothing in our lives can go forward without choosing to obey God. God's not going to give us more revelation if we didn't obey the last revelation He gave us.

I hear a lot of Christians say they don't know how to hear God. I wonder how many of them didn't obey when they did hear. I want to say, "Go back to the last thing you heard God say that you didn't obey and do that. Then, maybe God will speak again."

One Step At A Time

Sometimes God only gives us direction one step at a time. Don't let the unknown of what the second step might be stop you from ever taking the first step. You may never know what God would have done if you don't take that first step of faith.

What if fear of the second step had kept Peter from taking the first step out of his boat?

He never would have walked on water. Peter had every reason to be afraid. People who get out of a boat at night during a storm in the middle of the lake typically sink. And Peter was no exception. His first step was nothing short of a miracle. But, his second step nearly drowned him. But, he didn't drown. Jesus reached out His hand and caught him. Yes, Jesus rebuked Peter for his lack of faith. People who walk on water sometimes lose faith... but they also get to walk on water! For one glorious moment they experience the impossible. They get to touch the supernatural hand of God. When Jesus told Peter to come to Him, Peter obeyed and it resulted in the miraculous.

You see, it's when we respond to the initiation of God that we get results. This is the third step to knowing God. Responding to God gets results. Genesis 12:2-3 tells us all that Abram would have forfeited if he hadn't obeyed.

"I will make you into a great nation and I will bless you; I will make your name great, and you will be a blessing. I will bless those who bless you, and whoever curses you I will curse; and all peoples on earth will be blessed through you."

You may be thinking, "Who wouldn't obey under those conditions?" But, Abram was 75 years old when God spoke to him. He had to load up all his possessions and leave what was familiar to him and his family. They had to give up their home and friends and start all over.

Would you pack up all your stuff and leave your home, family and friends to follow God?

Knowing God and experiencing His presence comes with a price. God initiates, we respond and it results in blessing in our lives.

The most significant blessing from God is the presence of God.

The manifest presence of God isn't something to trifle with. God is not a man to be ignored. Yet, that is what most of us do. Only those who respond to the "inward longing" will truly abide in God's presence.

Learning to Abide

1. Which of the three keys do you need to grow in the most?

2. What steps of action do you need to take to grow in your weakest area?

3. What are the promises of God for your life?

4. Do any of these promises mean more to you than God's presence?

5. Are there certain times in your life when you question if God's presence is really with you?

6. What is the biggest distraction that keeps you from God's presence?

7. How can you be more responsive to God?

8. Are there areas of disobedience in your life?

9. Are you willing to be obedient?

-6-
THE MANIFEST PRESENCE OF GOD

Did you know that there is a vast difference between God's presence and God's manifest presence? God is always present with us, but He doesn't always manifest His presence. He doesn't always make it evident that He is there. He doesn't always speak or act. Sometimes He's just there... silent and still.

It's like this: have you ever been in the same room with someone who doesn't say or do anything? They're just sitting there next to you. Then suddenly they begin to speak to you or ask you something. That person just manifested themselves. They just made it clear that they were in the room. They just made themselves obvious. Suddenly they are noticeable. Even though they were right there all along, they just made their presence apparent.

This is exactly what God does. He's there all the time, but He doesn't always manifest His presence. When He does, it is our responsibility to respond. What do you think would happen to our friends if we didn't respond when they spoke to us? What if we just sat there ignoring them, acting as though they weren't even there? Eventually they would quit coming around. They would make themselves scarce.

Fortunately God never leaves us or forsakes us.

He is always with us. There isn't anywhere we can go that God is not there. Wherever we are, wherever we go, whatever we do... God is with us. He is always a prayer away.

The Night Everything Changed

I'll never forget the first time God manifested Himself to me. It was during one of the most painful times of my life. As I previously mentioned, I was sexually abused by my stepfather when I was a child. This had been occurring for several years. As each year went by, I became more and more hopeless that it would ever end. I had tried everything to make it stop. I would avoid him as much as possible. I knew he would wait until my mother was at work, so I tried to hide out in my room at these times. If he came to my bedroom door I would pretend I was asleep or I would stay outside long after dark playing with my friends, hoping with everything in me that he wouldn't call me home. I also tried begging and pleading with him. But nothing worked. As hard as I tried I couldn't stop the abuse.

I was raised in Detroit, Michigan and the winters were intolerably cold. One of my favorite things to do was to curl up on the floor next to the heat vent. I would place a blanket over the vent and force the warm air to blow over me. I was covered in my blanket from head to toe. My stepfather's favorite place of abuse was our cold basement. So I found comfort in the contrast my bedroom floor provided; snuggled in the warmth of my blanket. This became my only escape after the cold, cruel basement episode.

This was my ritual, night after night, month after month, year after year. My nightmare would commence with the "basement episode" and conclude on my bedroom floor next to the heat vent.

Then, one night everything changed. I had returned to my bedroom after being abused. I was feeling so ashamed and alone. There on my bedroom floor for the first time in my life I prayed a silent prayer, a prayer that altered my life forever, perhaps the most significant prayer I ever prayed. "If there is a God, please don't ever let this happen again." The words welled up from deep within my child's heart as the tears fell from my swollen eyes. For the first time in my life I had prayed.

What happened next is as miraculous as that prayer. No sooner had my prayer ascended to heaven than I heard a knock on my bedroom door. My stepfather cracked the door open and said, "I'm not going to do this anymore."

That moment I knew there was a God. As long as I live I will never forget how that felt. I prayed and God answered. The warmth of my blanket sanctuary was freezing cold in comparison to the flaming fire of God's presence in my heart.

Others had told me God was real. At Vacation Bible School I heard stories about God. But, at this moment, I was experiencing Him for myself. I could feel Him, sense Him and almost touch Him. For the first time in my life I knew God was there. I knew He was there in the cold, dark basement that imprisoned me for so long. I knew He was there when I voiced my silent prayer. I knew He was there when I heard a knock on my bedroom door and my stepfather promised never to abuse me again. God had been there all along... I just hadn't realized it until now.

When You Least Expect It

In Genesis 27 and 28 we read about Isaac and Rebekah and their two sons Esau and Jacob. Esau was the firstborn and therefore he was entitled to the blessing of his father. But, their mother Rebekah convinced Jacob to steal Esau's blessing.

Jacob did as his mother demanded. He deceived his father Isaac and took his brother's blessing. When Esau learned that his brother had taken his blessing he plotted to kill him. When Rebekah learned that Esau was planning to kill his brother, she told Jacob to flee to the land of Haran where her brother Laban lived. So Jacob does what his mother tells him and he hightails it out of Beersheba and sets out for the land of Haran.

Along his journey Jacob decides to get some shut eye. While he sleeps he has a dream. In his dream, he sees a stairway resting on the earth, with its top reaching to heaven and the angels of God were ascending and descending on it. Then, God speaks to Jacob in his dream. In Genesis 28:12-15 He promises him that he and his descendants will inherit the land. They will be like the dust of the earth which will spread out to the West, the East, the North and the South and that all the people on the earth will be blessed through his offspring. He tells Jacob that He is with him and will watch over him wherever he goes. He promises to bring Jacob back to his land and to be with him until all these promises come to pass.

I can only imagine that when Jacob laid down to sleep his thoughts drifted to the events of that day. First, he betrayed his father and his brother. He stole Esau's blessing. As a result, he was forced to flee to a strange land so his brother wouldn't kill him. Now he's lying on the cold hard ground with a stone for a pillow.

I seriously doubt Jacob expected God to show up in his dreams. After everything that happened, he probably wasn't expecting God to be anywhere in sight. But when Jacob awakes from his dreamy sleep he is struck with the realization of God's unexpected visitation. He thinks to himself, "Surely the Lord is in this place, and I was not aware of it."

God was there all along, but Jacob didn't realize it until God spoke to him in a dream. God manifested Himself to Jacob and everything changed. Jacob declared, "How awesome is this place. This is none other than the house of God; this is the gate of heaven."

God was with Jacob all along, but Jacob didn't realize it until God manifested His presence.

It's More Than Just Shared Real Estate

Abiding in God's presence is more than just occupying the same space as God. It's more than just sharing real estate. It's about making a deliberate, purposeful, and determined effort to experience God throughout your day, moment by moment, amid the chaos, the interruptions, and the distractions. You don't let anything keep you from God. It's about finding God right where you are. And when God tries to get your attention, you respond. You stop what you're doing and you listen. If you can't stop what you're doing, you listen anyway.

Think for a moment about how many times a day you pick up your cell phone and call your loved ones. If they don't answer your call, you leave a message. If they don't get your voice message, you send a text message. If they are hard to contact, you keep trying.

Well, God isn't hard to contact. He's only a prayer away. All you have to do is call on Him. Call on Him in worship, call on Him by reading His Word and call on Him in prayer. And He won't ignore your call. He won't put you on hold. You don't have to leave a voice message. You are God's priority. Pick up the phone, make

Abide

the call. God is right there waiting.

Worship, the Word and prayer: three keys to abiding in God's presence. Now that we understand that the purpose of these keys is to abide in God's presence, let's continue our journey by examining "The Three Keys to Abiding in Christ."

Learning to Abide

1. Have you ever experienced the manifest presence of God? If yes, explain.

2. When was the last time God manifested Himself to you?

3. What happened that caused you to be aware of God's presence?

4. What can you do to cultivate your awareness of God's presence?

5. What are some ways you could make an effort to experience God in your life?

-7-
THE FIRST KEY IS ABIDING IN WORSHIP

John 15:7 says *If you abide in Me...* To abide in Jesus means to live where He lives. Psalms 22:3 says *God inhabits the praises of His people.* The word "inhabit" means "to dwell." So if God inhabits our praises and inhabit means "to dwell" then we can safely say that God lives in our praise and worship. So, when we worship we are dwelling (or abiding) with Him.

Your Worthship

So, what does it mean to worship? The word worship comes from an Old English word – "worthship" - which means "to attribute worth to someone." This word was used to address royalty. When someone of royal status would enter a room everyone would bow down and say, "Your worthship." In the same way, when the King of Kings enters the room our response should be to bow down and cry out in worship to Him.

You see, worship is experiencing the presence of God and responding appropriately. *Webster's Dictionary* defines worship as: extreme devotion, intense love or admiration. It's not something we do just on Sunday morning. It's is a lifestyle. We abide in worship. We don't have to be in church to worship God; our hearts can be a private place where we commune with Him moment by moment. Remember, abide means occupying a dwelling place. It means the place where we live. So, when we abide in Christ we dwell or live in a place of worship. We don't worship God from a distance. No, we dwell or abide right where He is.

Pitching A Tent

Exodus 33 tells a story that perfectly illustrates this. The Children of Israel were traveling to the Promised Land. Along the way they would stop and set up camp. Moses would go outside the camp and set up the Tent of Meeting. Exodus 33:8-11 says:

And whenever Moses went out to the tent, all the people rose and stood at the entrances to their tents, watching Moses until he entered the tent. As Moses went into the tent the pillar of cloud would come down and stay at the entrance, while the Lord spoke with Moses. Whenever the people saw the pillar of cloud standing at the entrance to the tent, they all stood and worshiped each at the entrance to his tent. The Lord would speak to Moses face to face, as a man speaks with his friend.

I want you to notice that verse 8 says, *all the people rose and stood at the entrances to their tents.*

Again in verse 10 it says, *they all stood and worshiped each at the entrance to his tent.*

Abide

The Children of Israel stood at their tent door instead of going into the tabernacle where God dwelt. They worshiped from afar.

But where was Moses? Verse 9 says Moses *went into the tent.* This was the tabernacle where God dwelt. Moses didn't worship from a distance. He went into the tent where God was. He dwelt where God dwelt. The children of Israel stood at their tent doors but Moses ENTERED INTO the tabernacle.

**The Children of Israel were Tent Door Worshipers.
Moses was a Tabernacle Worshiper.**

No wonder verse 11 says, *The Lord would speak to Moses face to face, as a man speaks with his friend.* Many of us are worshipping God at our tent door. Instead of drawing near, we stay at a distance and try to worship God. Fortunately, unlike the Children of Israel, we don't have to go to a tent to worship God. We have the Spirit of God living in us. But, figuratively we're still worshipping at our tent door. You see:

- Tent door worshipers don't have a passion for God's presence.

- Tent door worshipers are satisfied with worshipping God once a week on Sunday.

- Tent door worshipers stroll into church late on Sundays and really don't get much out of it.

- Tent door worshipers only worship if they feel like it.

- Tent door worshipers are more concerned about what others think than what God thinks. They wonder, "What will people think if I raise my hands or dance or shout?"

- Tent door worshipers worship their way, not God's way.

- Tent door worshipers like to complain about the worship... the music was too loud or not loud enough or they don't like the song choices.

On the other hand:

- Tabernacle worshipers have a passion to abide in God's presence.

- Tabernacle worshipers prime the pump for Sunday worship because they worship all week long.

- Tabernacle worshipers care more about what God thinks than what people think.

- Tabernacle worshipers worship God's way as prescribed in His Word.

- Tabernacle worshipers are usually on time for church because they treasure every moment of corporate worship.

- Tabernacle worshipers have a passion for God's presence that overrides personal preferences. They just want to worship God, no matter what.

- Tabernacle worshipers enter into God's presence.

- Tabernacle worshipers understand Psalms 27:4:

One thing I have asked from the Lord, that I shall seek. That I may dwell (or abide) in the house of the Lord all the days of my life. To behold the beauty of the Lord and to meditate in His temple.

So I ask you today... are you a Tent Door Worshiper or are you a Tabernacle Worshiper?

Do you stand at a distance - holding back - or do you enter into His presence? What does your worship look like on a daily basis? Do you get up each day, go your own way, make your own plans and live your life for yourself? Is God off in the distance waiting for you to acknowledge Him? Do you go to work and never give God a single thought? In your busyness do you ignore the still small voice vying for your attention? Are you distracted with everything you need to do? At night do you fall into bed without praying, asleep before your head even hits the pillow? Do you go through the whole day never speaking a word to God? Is God a distant stranger in your life? If so, then you are a Tent Door Worshiper.

Or are you a Tabernacle Worshiper? Do you wake up eager to meet with God? Do you include Him in your thoughts? Do you acknowledge Him in your day? Do you listen for His voice? Do you see Him in the people you meet? Do you recognize His goodness in the ordinary opportunities that come your way? Do you commune with Him despite the busyness of your day? Do you thank Him, share your feelings with Him, and spend time with Him? Then you are a Tabernacle Worshiper. What about church on Sunday? Do you go? Do you go regularly? Do you serve? Do you tithe? Do you enter into worship? Do you give God your best? Do you listen to the sermon? Do you respond to the sermon? Or are you just doing your religious duty? Are you just tolerating church? Or would you rather be home sleeping? Do you give God your best?

Watered Down Worship

There is a legend about an ancient village in Spain. The villagers learned that the king would pay a visit. In a thousand years, a king had never come to that village. Excitement grew. "We must throw a big celebration!" The villagers all agreed. But, it was a poor village, and there weren't many resources.

Someone came up with an idea. Since most of the villagers made their own wines, the idea was for everyone in the village to bring a large cup of their choice wine to the town square. They said, "We'll pour it into a large vat and offer it to the king for his pleasure! When the king draws wine to drink, it will be the very best he's ever tasted."

On the day of the king's arrival, people lined up to make their offering to the honored guest. They climbed a small stairway, and poured their gift through a small opening at the top until the vat was full. The king was escorted in with much fanfare, given a silver cup and was told to draw some wine, which represented the best the villagers had. He placed the cup under the spigot, turned the handle, and then drank the wine. The king got a very puzzled expression on his face and said, "This wine tastes exactly like water." You know why? Because it was!

You see, every villager reasoned, "I'm poor and cannot afford to give the king my best. I'll withhold my wine and substitute water. With so many cups of wine in the vat, the king will never know the difference!" The problem was, everyone thought the same thing, and the offering to the king ended up being a disappointing watered-down version.

That's what happens when we come to church expecting others to do the praising and ministering and giving: it waters down our worship.

If we have a passive person here and there or someone refusing to serve here and there, it waters down our worship and our ministry. If all of us wait for someone else to do the praising, no one will do the praising and our King will not be honored!

That's what happens when we're Tent Door Worshipers: it waters down our worship. If we have a bunch of Tent Door Worshipers who haven't worshiped all week long, who are standing at a distance expecting the Tabernacle Worshipers to do all the praising, it waters down our worship and our King will not be honored! No wonder going to church is drudgery for some people.

Today you can choose to be a Tabernacle Worshiper. You can begin tonight when you go to bed. Let your last words be words of prayer. Let your last thoughts be towards God. Tomorrow when you wake up, before your feet hit the floor, let your first words be words of prayer. Let your first thoughts be towards God. This Sunday when you go to church, give it all you've got. Pay attention to the sermon. Sign up to serve in a needed area. Give it all you've got. Be a Tabernacle Worshiper.

Abide

Learning to Abide

1. Are you a Tent Door Worshiper or a Tabernacle Worshiper?

2. List some ways you distance yourself in worship.

3. What is one thing you can do to draw closer to God in worship?

-8-

THE SECOND KEY IS ABIDING IN GOD'S WORD

John 15:7 says *If you abide in Me, and My words abide in you...*

Bible Thumper

As Christians we are supposed to be people of the Word: Bible-reading, Bible-believing followers of Christ. I know people who say, "I believe every word of the Bible," yet they hardly ever read it!

According to the Library of Congress, during a typical week only 45% of American Christians read the Bible. Of the 45%, just 12% claim to read God's Word daily and 55% don't even bother to open it once a week!

If the only Bible teaching you get is what you get on Sunday – you're spiritually starving.

That would be like eating one meal a week and wondering why you have no strength. Hearing preaching and teaching on Sunday is necessary, but it is also necessary to feed ourselves. George Barna's research shows what happens when we don't study God's Word:

- 60% of Americans can't name five of the Ten Commandments.

Abide

- 82% of Americans think the saying, "God helps those who help themselves," is a Bible verse.
- 12% believe Joan of Arc was Noah's wife.
- Many people think the Sermon on the Mount was preached by Billy Graham.
- 25% don't know what we celebrate on Easter.

No wonder Christians are living less and less like Christ. We know less and less of the Word. We will never believe more than we know. We will never abide where we don't go. We will never be what we can't see. We must see Christ in His Word if we are to be as Christ in the world. 2 Timothy 3:16-17 says:

All Scripture is given by inspiration of God, and is profitable for doctrine, for reproof, for correction, for instruction in righteousness, that the man of God may be complete, thoroughly equipped for every good work.

The word "complete" means mature.

You will never grow to spiritual maturity apart from abiding in the Word.

We all know the Scripture, *You shall know the truth and the truth will make you free.* But do we know what comes before that – what freedom is contingent upon? John 8:31-32 says:

If you continue in My word, then are you My disciples indeed, and you shall know the truth, and the truth shall make you free.

Change comes as we continue in the Word. The word "continue" is the Greek word "meno" which means abide. Remember abide means to live there! So basically this passage is saying, "If you live in God's Word you will be free." Or you could say it like this: change comes as you live in God's Word.

Whatever you need from God comes through abiding in His Word.

Notice that Jesus said those who abide in His Word are His disciples. Abiding in the Word is more than occasionally reading your Bible. Abiding in the Word is more than hearing a sermon once a week. Abiding in the Word means to read the Word regularly and then to meditate on the Word, which means to think about it through the day. Joshua 1:8 says:

Do not let this Book of the Law depart from your mouth; meditate on it day and night, so that you may be careful to do everything written in it. Then you will be prosperous and successful.

Notice that successful people don't just read the Bible; they meditate on it, they think about it, they speak it, they do it and they live it. They live in the Word for knowing and for growing. They live in the Word for perceiving and for believing. They live in the Word for information and for transformation.

Those who abide in God's Word will never make a decision without consulting God's Word first.

Bible Junkie

People who abide in the Word make the Word of God their plumb line. Everything is measured by the Word of God. They're Bible junkies, addicted to every word in the Bible. They hunger and thirst for the righteousness that is found in the pages of the Bible. They seek for God on every page. The written Word leads them to the living Word: Jesus. They would rather die than be deprived of the Word. It is their joy, their peace, their existence. Nothing equals the impact of the Word in their life. Everything else pales in comparison.

In contrast, immature Christians live on spiritual junk food. They would rather listen to Oprah or read a romance novel or flip through the pages of People magazine. They spend more time on Facebook than they do in God's book. Then, they wonder why they have no strength, no wisdom, no direction, no life or no growth. They need to get off Facebook and get their face in God's book! In order to grow as Christians we need to get God's Word off our shelves and into ourselves. We must read it for it to feed us. There is no magic in the Bible. There is no "instant maturity."

Christian growth comes through hard-core, deliberate determination to read and obey the Word.

Here's what happens when you abide in God's Word: when you're down it will lift you up!

When you're lost, it will show you the way! When you're fearful, it will give you courage! When you're hurting, it will give you healing! When you're weak, it will give you strength! When you doubt, it will build your faith! When you're in despair, it will give you hope! When you're spiritually hungry, it will feed you! When you feel spiritually dead, it will give you life!

If you want to know God, you must abide in worship, you must abide in the Word and lastly, you must abide in prayer.

Learning to Abide

1. How many days a week do you read your Bible?

2. List some areas of your life where you need to grow spiritually.

3. How would reading your Bible help you grow where you are spiritually weak?

-9-
THE THIRD KEY IS ABIDING IN PRAYER

John 15:7 says, *If you abide in Me, and My words abide in you, you will ask what you desire, and it shall be done for you.*

A City Without Shoes

A traveler arrived in a city one cold morning. As he stepped off the train he noticed that everything appeared normal except everyone was barefooted. No one wore shoes. Hurriedly, he hailed a cab and the cab driver didn't have on shoes. So he asked the driver, "I was just wondering why you're not wearing shoes. Don't you believe in shoes?" "Yes, that's the question," the driver replied. "Why don't we wear shoes?"

The same thing happened at the hotel. No one wore shoes. Not the door man or the bell boy. It was the same in the coffee shop. A man drinking coffee had no shoes. So the traveler asked him, "I noticed you aren't wearing any shoes. Don't you know about shoes?" The man replied, "Of course I know about shoes." The traveler asked, "Then why don't you wear them?" And the answer was, "That is the question: why don't we wear them?"

The traveler walked out into the snowy street and everybody was barefooted. He asked a

Abide

bystander why no one had shoes on. "Doesn't anyone in this town believe in shoes?" The bystander turned to him and said, "Yes, we know about shoes and we believe in shoes. See that building over there? That is a shoe factory and every week we gather there to hear a man tell us how wonderful shoes are."

"Then, why don't you wear shoes?" asked the visitor. "Yes, that is the question," was the answer. The man walked away shaking his head in amazement at a city full of people who believed in shoes, but never wore them.

The same thing could be said about the church and prayer. Do we believe in prayer? Sure we do. Do we know what it could mean in our lives? Of course we do. Do we gather to learn about prayer? Yes. Then, why don't we pray? Yes, that is the question.

You see, the tragic dilemma of today's church is not unanswered prayer but unoffered prayer.

Too Busy Not To Pray

One of the most common excuses for not praying is busyness. I like what Martin Luther said about that: "When I have a busy day I pray one hour. When I have a really busy day I pray two hours." Most of us would say the exact opposite. The busier we are the less we pray. Some days we're doing good to pray at all. We've grown accustomed to prayerlessness. But why?

Why don't we pray? Why is it so hard to pray? Why does prayer seem like drudgery so much of the time?

That is the question and I think I know part of the answer: maybe we don't pray because we see prayer as something we have to do instead of Someone we get to know. Prayer becomes a discipline that leaves us feeling bored and unfulfilled. We approach God with an obligatory mental list of religious requests that seem appropriate and necessary. We come to God with a checklist of prayers that seem logical and spiritual. Prayer is reduced to a religious duty.

But we are totally missing the essence of prayer. God doesn't want our mental gymnastics of reasoning or performance. He isn't playing spiritual mind games. He doesn't expect you to figure out all the right answers to satisfy His unreasonable demands. No! A thousand times no! God wants you. He wants your heart. He wants you to tell Him your innermost thoughts, your fears, your pain, your worries, your sorrows, and your disappointments. He wants you to tell Him when you're angry or lonely or overwhelmed. He also wants you to share your joys and the things that make you happy. God wants you to share your feelings with Him. Good or bad.

Heart To Heart

When I began to understand that prayer was about sharing my heart with God, it revolutionized my relationship with Him. Suddenly, prayer became natural. When I felt sad I would tell God. When I was worried I would share that with Him too. No masks, no pretense. It was just me and God. I would share my heart with Him and He would meet me there.

Never once has He shamed me or condemned me. He has only, always, tenderly loved me more. Sharing heart to heart with Him has become the greatest, most meaningful, pleasurable part of every day. Pouring my heart out to God - unashamedly, freely, honestly and openly - is my delight. And when God speaks to me and touches me I am undone. I am lovesick and I know what the Shulamite woman in Song of Solomon meant when she uttered, "His love is better than wine." Listen to this prayer of intimacy with God in Song of Solomon 1:2-4:

Let Him kiss me with the kisses of His mouth for Your love is more delightful than wine. Pleasing is the fragrance of Your perfumes; Your name is like perfume poured out. No wonder the maidens love You! Take me away with You — let us hurry! Let the King bring me into His chambers. We rejoice and delight in You; we will praise Your love more than wine.

Why don't we pray? It's because we don't really understand what prayer is. When we begin to understand, we won't be able to stop praying. It will become as natural as breathing. We will shout it to the heavens: *Take me away with You — let us hurry!*

Dare I Ask?

Once we experience God in prayer it's not difficult to ask for what we need. We will stop expecting God to bless us without having to ask. It doesn't work that way. God wants us to ask. John 15:7 says:

Ask what you desire, and it shall be done for you.

If we want something from God we must ask. The word "ask" in this verse is the Greek word "aieto." According to *Kittles Theological Dictionary of the New Testament*, one of the meanings of "aieto" is "to demand or request." Think about that. God's Word is saying it's okay to be demanding when we ask.

When I think about being demanding, I usually don't equate that with prayer. As a matter of fact, those are the last two words I would use to describe my prayers to God. But God is saying we can be demanding when we approach the throne of grace.

Now, before you think I'm a lunatic or a heretic, let me explain. I'm not saying we should be rude or arrogant in prayer. As a matter of fact, the word "aiteo" is used to depict a person addressing a superior. The person may be insistent, but it is done with the utmost respect. This word involves an expectation of receiving. It leaves no doubt that abiding in prayer earns us the right to pray authoritatively and to expect - even demand - to receive.

Take, for example, the widow who demanded that the unjust judge give her justice against her adversary. Time after time she went to him demanding that he grant her request. Luke 18:4-8 tells the outcome.

For some time he refused. But finally he said to himself, 'Even though I don't fear God or care about men, yet because this widow keeps bothering me, I will see that she gets justice, so that she won't eventually wear me out with her coming!' And the Lord said, "Listen to what the unjust judge says. And will not God bring about justice for His chosen ones, who cry out to Him day and night? Will He keep putting them off? I tell you, He will see that they get justice, and quickly. However, when the Son of Man comes, will He find faith on the earth?"

One day I was sharing this concept with a young woman I mentor. I was struggling to give her an example of a situation where we could demand something of God. Instead, she gave me an example: a very poignant and personal example from her own life. She had been a believer for three years, but before she was saved she lived a homosexual lifestyle. Her story defines what it means to demand something from God. Here's her story:

"Demanding that God remove this sin from my life was not a one-time occurrence, but I remember the night it started. I had been struggling with homosexuality my whole life. The plans I had made for my life were going nowhere and it had been that way for a long time. I had been inside a bookstore digging through a stack of books when I came across a book that dealt with freedom from homosexuality. I just knew this book was the key to my deliverance. I could hardly wait to start reading.

'That evening, alone in my bedroom, I began to read. I was so certain that this book would give me the answers I had been seeking for so long. But my hopes quickly turned to despair. Before I finished the introduction the author stated that being free from homosexuality was uncommon and practically impossible. Not only would this be the hardest thing I ever tried, it was likely I would fail.

I slammed the book shut and began to cry... but my tears brought a new resolve. I refused to believe that I would have to fight this sin my whole life. I knew God had a destiny for me that included freedom from my past.

'That moment I chose to believe what God said instead of what man said. I felt a boldness rise up in me and I began to demand that God deliver me from homosexuality: "No! I will not live like this," I spoke out loud. "I will be free. You will set me free. I do not want this. Take this from me," I demanded of God."

And God did take homosexuality from her! He honored her demands. Why? First, because she asked. Secondly, because she asked according to His will. I John 5:14-15 says:

This is the confidence we have in approaching God: that if we ask anything according to His will, He hears us. And if we know that He hears us - whatever we ask - we know that we have what we asked of Him.

You see, we can't just arbitrarily ask whatever we want and think that God is obligated to answer our prayer. Our prayers must reflect God's will for our lives.

Thirdly, God answered her prayer because she was abiding. She didn't just ask one time and go her merry way. She stayed up all night crying out to God over and over and over. She dug her heals in and repeatedly petitioned God. And she didn't stop there. Even though God delivered her that day, she still has areas of her life that need healing from the devastating effects of living a homosexual lifestyle. Yes, God delivered her, but He is still setting her free on a daily basis. We must ask according to God's will and keep on asking. This is how we abide in prayer and those who abide have the privilege of answered prayer.

A Kitchen, An Apron And A Closet

1 Thessalonians 5:17 says to *pray without ceasing*. Brother Lawrence, a great man of God in the 1600's, was a great example of this. He was known for his intimacy with God and peace in his life. His secret was knowing how to abide

in prayer even though he spent most of his life working in a kitchen. He believed that he cooked meals, ran errands, and scrubbed pots... alongside God.

One of his most famous sayings refers to his kitchen: "I began to live as if there were no one save God and me in the world. The time of business does not with me differ from the time of prayer; and in the noise and clatter of my kitchen, while several persons are at the same time calling for different things; I still possess God in as great tranquility as if I were upon my knees..."

Susanna Wesley was the mother of nineteen children, including John and Charles Wesley who were the founders of the Methodist Movement. John preached over 40,000 sermons about a personal relationship with God. Susanna had one goal as a mother: to raise her children to honor God and live for eternity in heaven. Her secret to accomplishing this was her God and her apron.

Susanna knew the importance of abiding, so when she needed to pray she pulled her apron over her head. Her children knew not to disturb her if her apron was over her head. Unless you have more than nineteen children you have no excuse for not abiding in prayer.

When my children were little I really struggled finding time to pray. I was easily distracted and when I tried to pray I would think of a million things that needed to be done. So I set up a prayer closet in our master bedroom closet. I had an altar, a Bible, a CD player and a box of Kleenex. When I would close the closet door it was as if I was instantly transported into the heavens. I would pray and cry and read the Word and pray some more and listen to worship CD's and worship my heart out. That closet floor was my sanctuary.

Years later we moved. Then I found my sanctuary at my kitchen table. My children were in school and I would sit at our kitchen table for hours praying, worshiping and reading my Bible.

Today my meeting place with God is my desk in my office. I now listen to worship music on my Mini IPad, write in my journal and talk to God. I've always had a designated place that I go to seek God. It helps me stay disciplined. It keeps me on track.

But I don't have to go to "my place" to meet God because I can meet with God no matter where I am. I meet with Him in the sanctuary of my heart. I commune with Him from within. I do this because He abides in me and I abide in Him.

When we abide in prayer there is an exchange:

- I exchange my fear for His faith
- I exchange my anger for His peace
- I exchange my depression for His joy

- I exchange my weakness for His strength

I change my address: the place where I live or abide. I no longer live in fear, anger, depression, or weakness. I now live in faith, peace, joy and strength. But the key to this kind of praying is in the first part of this verse... *IF you abide in Me, and My words abide in you.*

You see, Christ knew that if His Word lives in us we will never ask for something that is out of line with His will. That's what gives us the authority to "aiteo" or adamantly request something of God. "Aiteo" seizes God's will for our life and respectfully demands that it be manifested. Hebrews 4:16 says:

Let us therefore come boldly to the throne of grace that we may obtain mercy and find grace to help in time of need.

That Takes A Lot Of Nerve

In Luke 11:5-10, Jesus told a parable about boldness:

Suppose one of you has a friend, and he goes to him at midnight and says, "Friend, lend me three loaves of bread, because a friend of mine on a journey has come to me, and I have nothing to set before him."

In Bible times it was customary for travelers to come for bread at the midnight hour. Everyone knew the importance of having bread prepared.

To be out of bread meant this midnight seeker was unprepared, but he asked any way. Listen to the friend's response in verse 7:

Don't bother me. The door is already locked, and my children are with me in bed. I can't get up and give you anything.

The man told him no. But that's not the end of the story. Verse 8 says:

I tell you, though he will not get up and give him the bread because he is his friend, yet because of the man's boldness he will get up and give him as much as he needs.

Here's what I want you to see: even though the midnight seeker was unprepared, he had the boldness to go and ask for what he needed. And because he asked boldly, he received. Many preachers interpret his boldness to mean persistence. However, this word boldness in the Greek means "importunity." According to *Vine's Dictionary*, importunity means "shamelessness."

The lesson here revolves around one key thought. The reason the midnight seeker gets what he needs is not just because of his persistence. It's not just because of his friendship. It's because he had the nerve to ask.

It would take a lot of boldness to go to your friend's house at midnight and wake him up pounding on his door. You would have to set aside what is considered proper and normal protocol. The message of this parable is clear: God wants us to ask Him freely and boldly.

Boldness is our privilege.
We can approach God with unashamed forwardness.

We should never hesitate to pray because we feel unworthy or because we feel God is distant or because we are uncertain about how much to ask for. Jesus strikes a death blow to our hesitancy in Luke 11:9-10:

So I say to you: Ask and it will be given to you; seek and you will find; knock and the door will be opened to you. For everyone who asks receives; he who seeks finds; and to him who knocks, the door will be opened.

ASK – call on God to work in the midst of your circumstances. SEEK – pursue God with the determination of a starving man. KNOCK – strike the obstacle that is in your way, like the friend who pounded on the door and overcame the obstacle between him and his provision.

Boldness asks God and keeps asking until it receives. Boldness seeks and keeps seeking until it finds. Boldness knocks and keeps knocking until God opens the door.

Heaven's storehouse isn't in short supply.
God isn't rationing answers to prayer.

Dear child of God, at this very moment God is

listening to the cry of your heart. He is fully invested in hearing and answering your prayer. He is waiting patiently for you to turn to Him. He caused the sun to shine on you today. He sent the rain to refresh you. He intervened before you made a stupid mistake. He went before you. He is your rear guard. He enlarged your steps beneath you so your foot would not slip. He is ever ready and eager to answer, but you must ask. His angels are waiting for His command, but you must ask.

So, open your heart to Him. Bow your knee and humbly call out to Him. He is waiting. You won't be disappointed. You see prayer changes things.

- Hannah prayed and her barrenness became fruitfulness. (I Samuel 1:20)
- Jonah prayed and the fish spit him onto dry land. (Jonah 2:7 & 10)
- Elijah prayed and the heavens gave rain. (James 5:17-18)
- The disciples prayed and they were filled with the Holy Spirit. (Acts 4:31)
- Paul and Silas prayed and the prison doors flew open and everyone's chains were loosed. (Acts 16:25-27)

Prayer Changes Things

Remember the words God spoke to Jeremiah: you will seek Me and find Me when you seek Me with all your heart. Remember the words of Paul in I Thessalonians 5:17? He didn't say sing without ceasing or fellowship without ceasing or even preach without ceasing. He said, *"Pray without ceasing."*

In Luke 11:1, the disciples said to Jesus, *"Teach us to pray."* Immediately after that request, Jesus taught two parables on prayer: the parable about the widow and the judge and the parable about the midnight seeker who asks for bread. We've already seen that the parable about the midnight seeker is about bold prayer.

The parable about the widow and the judge can be summed up in three words: "Don't give up." Two primary truths that Jesus taught about prayer are: be bold and don't give up. Keep on praying! James 5:16 says:

The effective, fervent prayer of a righteous man avails much.

The word effective comes from a Greek word that means "a fixed position." If you want your prayers to be effective you must state your position and refuse to move until God answers.

Worship, the Word and prayer are the three keys to abiding. If you want to succeed in life, abide in worship, the Word and prayer. If you want to succeed in marriage, abide in worship, the Word and prayer. If you want to succeed against the enemy, abide in worship, the Word and prayer.

I encourage you to abide in worship. Not just on Sundays, but every day of the week. Live in

Abide

God's presence. Be a Tabernacle Worshiper. Don't worship God from a distance. Enter His gates with thanksgiving and into His courts with praise. And don't let a day go by without praying to God.

Call on Him when you're down. Call on Him when you're happy. Call on Him when life is tough. Call on Him when life is good. Call on Him when you feel like it. Call on Him when you don't feel like it. When you call on Him, He will answer and He will show you great and mighty things. He will change your life, defeat your enemies, give you victory, fill you with joy, renew your purpose, heal your marriage, and restore what you've lost.

Yes, prayer changes things, but more importantly, prayer changes us!

But in order for that change to happen, you must get in His Word and let His Word get in you. You must be a Bible-reading and Bible-believing child of God. Then, when the hard times come, His Word will rise up in you to strengthen you and encourage you. If you want to abide, you must get in His Word, worship and pray. There's no other way.

Learning to Abide

1. What does it mean to you to share your heart with God in prayer?

2. List the prayer requests that you are adamantly believing God for.

3. What is your biggest hindrance to unceasing prayer?

4. What are you willing to do to be persistent and bold in prayer?

Abide

SECTION THREE

THE HINDRANCES TO ABIDING IN CHRIST

Abide

-10-
IT'S THE LITTLE FOXES

If Only

Anyone who wants to go forward in life must be willing to look backward. I'm not talking about living in the past or rehearsing regrets. That's not the purpose of looking back.

We look back so we can learn from our mistakes and move forward.

All of us need to evaluate where we are in life, where we want to be and how we plan to get there. It's important to measure our successes and our failures, our wins and our losses, our set-backs and our advancements. It's important to examine our past and learn from it. It's important to take an inventory of our mistakes so we don't repeat them. It's important to learn from our failures and as John Maxwell says, "Fail Forward."

Most of us are acutely aware of the mistakes that we've made. They're tucked away in our memory bank and accessed frequently and with ease. They haunt us like a ghost in the night. They're a constant reminder of our failure. They usually begin with the words "if only" or "I should have." They hover in the corners of our minds like a dark cloud on a stormy day. They loom in our thoughts bigger than life itself.

Abide

If only I had gone to college.
If only I hadn't invested my money that way.
If only I hadn't quit my job.
If only I hadn't divorced my wife.
If only I had spent more time with my kids.
If only I hadn't had an affair.
If only I hadn't got in so much debt.
If only I hadn't drank so much.
I should have saved more money.
I should have lost weight.
I should have gone to the doctor.
I should have gone to church.
I should have been a better parent or spouse or employee or friend.

These mistakes weren't little oversights. They were game changers. They were deal breakers. They were big mistakes; too big to overlook, hide or bury away.

If we're honest we'll admit that behind these big mistakes were even bigger causes and behind these bigger causes were even bigger sins like pride, rebellion, fear, unbelief, lust, selfishness, unforgiveness, and anger.

These big mistakes had big consequences. Maybe that's why it's so easy to remember the big mistakes. It's even easier to beat ourselves over the head for being so stupid. All of us make big mistakes and all of us suffer big time for those big mistakes.

But I don't want to talk about the big mistakes. We're already acutely aware of them. You don't need me to remind you of them. I probably can't tell you anything you don't already know about the big mistakes in your life. That's why I want to talk about the little mistakes. It was the little mistakes that most likely led to the big mistakes. It was the little sins that didn't seem so bad that led to bigger sins. It was the little behaviors that compounded over time and morphed into something that seemed too big to overcome.

A Thief In The Night

It's the little mistakes and the little sins that creep up like a thief in the night.

The little sins give birth and become the parents of the big ones.

They disguise themselves as normal and reasonable until they gain access to our souls and contaminate our spirits. They take up residence within our hearts, imprison our wills and take over our lives. Call it whatever you want: it's the little mistakes, the little sins, the little behaviors that catch us unaware.

If someone came up to you today and said, "You need to leave your spouse" or "You need to lie to your boss" or "You should go get drunk," you'd probably walk away. But, if you go to work every day and flirt with your co-worker or you exaggerate your performance to your boss or you make it a habit to go out drinking with the gang after work... if you do these seemingly little things over a period of time... eventually you probably will leave your spouse, lie and get drunk.

The little things we do become big hindrances in our lives. But, more importantly, they become hindrances to abiding in Christ and living in the presence of God. Song of Solomon 2:15 says it like this:

Catch for us the foxes, the little foxes that ruin the vineyards, our vineyards that are in bloom.

The little foxes are those hard-to-detect problems that quietly destroy relationships.

The little foxes exist to ruin our spiritual vineyards. According to the *Encarta Dictionary* the word "ruin" means "a state of complete destruction, decay, collapse, or loss." It can also mean complete devastation or complete failure. This failure can be moral, social or economic. John 10:10 says:

The thief comes only to steal and kill and destroy.

The little foxes are thieves assigned to devastate your life by stealing your blessings. They want to rob you of your hope, your joy, your dreams, your destiny, your faith, your relationships, your money, your health and anything else they can get their filthy hands on that belongs to you. They are Satan's undercover agents assigned to kill, annihilate and snuff the life out of everything you care about. Their one objective is to destroy you, burn you to the ground, and choke you to death. The little foxes want to ruin your vineyard.

The Cords Of Sin

According to *Strong's Concordance* the word "ruin" means "to bind (specifically by a pledge.)" It also means "to wind tightly (like a tightly wound rope)."

Here's what I think this means. If we don't rid our vineyard of the little foxes, we are inadvertently binding ourselves to our enemy. Without realizing it we've made a silent pledge with our adversary that gives him access to our vineyard. Once he's gained access he will bind his twisted rope of lies and deception around our neck until he chokes the life out of us. He'll ensnare us with the cords of sin until we can't breathe.

Proverbs 5:22-23 describes this condition:

His own iniquities entrap the wicked man, and he is caught in the cords of his sin. He shall die for lack of instruction, and in the greatness of his folly he shall go astray.

The *Bible in Basic English* says it like this:

The evil-doer will be taken in the net of his crimes, and prisoned in the cords of his sin. He will come to his end for need of teaching; he is so foolish that he will go wandering from the right way.

If Satan can't completely annihilate us, then he'll twist the truth with his lies until we are so stuck we don't know up from down, left from right, right from wrong or the truth from a lie. We may be alive, but we are like an animal caught in a trap. We're bound so tightly that we live a stressed out, uptight life of sin and deception.

You see, our little foxes aren't just little foxes. They are sins. And our sins will separate us from abiding in God's presence. We see this all the way back in the beginning when God punished Cain for killing his brother. Cain said this in Genesis 4:13-16:

"My punishment is more than I can bear. Today You are driving me from the land, and I will be hidden from Your presence." So Cain went out from the Lord's presence and lived in the land of Nod, east of Eden.

Our little foxes - called sins - separate us from abiding in God's presence.

Moses understood this. That's why when Israel sinned Moses prayed this prayer in Exodus 34:8-9:

Moses bowed to the ground at once and worshiped. "O Lord, if I have found favor in Your eyes," he said, "Then let the Lord go with us. Although this is a stiff-necked people, forgive our wickedness and our sin..."

If we want to abide in the presence of God, we

must repent of our sin. 1 John 1:9-10 says:

If we confess our sins, He is faithful and just and will forgive us our sins and purify us from all unrighteousness.

None of us will achieve sinless perfection in this lifetime. That's why we must confess our sins, be cleansed and live in righteousness.

We can't live any way we want and abide in God's presence at the same time.

We can't cohabit with our little foxes and expect everything to be okay. The consequences of allowing the little foxes access to our vineyard are inexhaustible. They can adversely impact every area of our lives.

Little By Little

One morning I was talking to my daughter on the phone. I wanted her opinion on what I was writing, so I asked her if I could read this chapter to her. Before the last words were out of my mouth she interjected, "That's what happened in my first marriage."

Kristen's first marriage ended in divorce after only four years. She's now remarried and about to celebrate her tenth anniversary. She went on to tell me that in her first marriage they didn't deal with all the little things. They didn't resolve the ongoing nuances and the small issues. Eventually, those small issues transformed into big issues and destroyed their marriage.

"That's why," Kristen continued, "I don't ever go to bed without dealing with stuff. I don't let the little things go because I know what will happen. They will become big things. That's just my belief."

Well it's God's belief too. Ephesians 4:26 says:

In your anger do not sin: Do not let the sun go down while you are still angry.

If you were to ask my daughter what contributed to the breakup of her first marriage, she would say it was the little things that eventually became big things. She would say the big difference between a failed marriage and a successful one is failing to deal with the little frustrations that grow into a huge chasm of pain and discouragement that eventually seem uncrossable.

Kristen's story shows us the importance of eradicating the little foxes. However, this is usually easier said than done. Why? Because we have to catch them. One of the characteristics of little foxes is their tendency to hide among the leaves in the vineyard. In ancient days they would infiltrate the vineyard and destroy the grapes. They derived their name from their habit of digging or burrowing underground. They were, cunning, subtle, sly and hard to detect until they had practically annihilated the crops.

Perhaps it's the little fox of mistrust and jealousy that builds walls between us and others. Or it may be the little fox of selfishness and pride which refuses to admit our faults to others. Or maybe it is unforgiveness that decays into bitterness toward others. Or maybe it is laziness, irresponsibility, passivity, lack of discipline, discouragement, a bad attitude, ungratefulness, complaining, exaggerating, or negativity. These little foxes have been ruining vineyards for years and if you let them, they will spoil your vineyard too.

Harvest Time Is Prime Time

According to *Easton's Bible Dictionary* these little foxes were also known as a plunderer of ripe grapes. Ripe grapes were the ones that were mature and ready to harvest. They are fully grown and ready to be picked.

You are never more vulnerable to the little foxes than when you are ready for harvest.

Just about the time God is going to bless you, those little foxes begin to manifest in your vineyard. They wait until after you've tilled the hard ground, removed the weeds, planted the tender seed, fertilized, watered, sprayed pesticides and worked your fingers to the bone. A bountiful crop is just waiting to be harvested. All your hard work is about to pay off.

This is when the sneaky little foxes devise their plan of attack. That's when Satan comes to pilfer your reward. He's patiently and strategically waited for this opportune time... right when you are about to reap what you've sown. Then, he strikes with the ferocity of a starving animal that will stop at nothing. He wants nothing more than to rob you of the fruit of your labor.

What better way to discourage you than to steal your reward.

The devil knows harvest time is the best time for an all-out assault. He knows this is when he can do the most damage. That's why he disguises himself among the tender new leaves, slowing gnawing away at them, careful not to devour them... until they are ripe.

As I mentioned earlier, my husband and I have been pastors at Grace Fellowship Church for over a decade. I love pastoring together and I'm living my dream. However, throughout the years I have noticed a pattern. Every time God is about to bless us with exponential increase, the little foxes begin to surface in my life. Without fail they rear their ugly heads and go on a feeding frenzy in my vineyard.

What's most distressing is that I gave them a certificate of occupancy. Not intentionally, but nonetheless, I gave them legal ground. How? Let me tell you how. As much as I love people there are some things people do that I hate. I hate it when people don't do what they say they're going to do. James 5:12 says:

Let your "Yes" be yes, and your "No," no, or you will be condemned.

I couldn't agree more. It's a biblical principle that if you say you're going to do something then you should do it. Now, I know there are some valid exceptions, but as a general rule we should do what we said we would do and follow through on what we commit to. If we say we will call, email or text someone, or volunteer to serve, or attend an event, or follow-up on a project... then we should do what we said we would do.

Unfortunately, not everyone shares my sentiments. It's become common place to *not do* what you say you will do.

As a pastor with a church of hundreds of people I encounter this scenario almost every day. And almost every day I find myself frustrated because of it. I know I shouldn't let it bother me, but the little foxes slink their way into my mind and erode away at my thoughts: "How can people be so inconsiderate? Don't they care about keeping their word? Don't they care that others were depending on them? Don't they care that I was depending on them?"

This is just one scenario that imprisons my thoughts. My other little foxes appear when people rebel against authority and won't admit they've made a mistake. Then, there's the little fox that nibbles away at my vineyard every time someone is late. This is a "big" little fox. One I'm well acquainted with.

Of course, I understand that there are mitigating circumstances for some of these situations. I'm agreeable when someone has a legitimate reason. But when these behaviors are chronic – which they usually are - I find myself conversing with my little foxes once again.

Lessons From A Frog

Now please understand I'm not bragging about my little foxes. I despise them. But, I'm also caught off guard by them. It's like a frog in a kettle. If you put a frog in a pot of hot water he will leap out immediately because he can tell that he's in danger. But, if you put him in a pot of room temperature water and slowly turn up the heat, he will stay in the water. He can't tell he's in danger. He can't tell that the water is getting hotter and he's about to be boiled to death. Instead of jumping out, he'll just stay in the kettle until he's dead.

Just like that frog, I'm surprisingly unaware of the devastation my little foxes are causing. That's when I find myself unable to enjoy the blessings of God in my life. God answers a prayer and instead of rejoicing I find myself skeptical or ungrateful. A door of opportunity opens and I hesitate to go forward. I'm burned out and all the little frustrations start erupting like a pot of boiling water. That's when I realize my vineyard is being plundered at harvest time.

So how do we catch the little foxes? We do what the bride did in Song of Solomon 2:15. She admitted she had a problem. Just the fact that she asked her bridegroom to catch her little foxes is evidence of her honesty. Her request alone reveals her vulnerability and transparency about her problems.

The first step towards identifying the problems in our relationship with God is to admit we have a problem.

It's impossible to solve a problem we don't admit we have.

Until we admit we have a problem we won't be able to get rid of it. Once we admit it, then we are ready to confess it and ask God's forgiveness. Only then can we protect our vineyard. 1 John 1:9-10 says:

If we confess our sins, He is faithful and just and will forgive us our sins and purify us from all unrighteousness. If we claim we have not sinned, we make Him out to be a liar and His word has no place in our lives.

After we've admitted our sins to God we must trust that He has forgiven us. Then and only then can we catch the little foxes. Or should I say, only then can God catch the little foxes. We must rely on God to catch the little foxes for us. That's what the bride in Song of Solomon did. She asked her bridegroom to solve her pesky problem and that's exactly what we must do. You see, the bride symbolizes all believers and the bridegroom symbolizes God. Therefore, we must ask God to catch our little foxes.

Out Of Your League

This wise woman obviously knew she was no match for these little foxes. She knew that apart from the vine she could do nothing to save their vineyard. She knew she was just a helpless, dangling branch waiting to be devoured. She knew that unless her bridegroom came to her rescue, she was doomed. She was wise enough to know that this assignment was beyond her ability.

This wise maiden also knew there was no time to waste. Her vineyard was at risk. She had to move quickly and precisely. She didn't waste any time trying figure out what to do. There was only one solution: her bridegroom must save her. Only he could rid her of the dangers threatening their relationship.

And the same is true of us. There isn't a strategy strategic enough. There isn't a plan thorough enough. There isn't a program insightful enough. There isn't a person wise enough. God and only God can save us from the little foxes.

Some of us have been nurturing our little foxes for so long that they aren't so little any more. Those little foxes are now big foxes in our lives. They are gigantic hindrances to abiding. They are massive, life threatening strongholds to our relationship with God and others.

The list of hindrances is inexhaustible: fear, phobias, shame, condemnation, guilt, loneliness, rejection, anger, unforgiveness, hopelessness, burnout, apathy, self-pity, unbelief, depression, discouragement, despair, impatience, pride, rebellion, overreacting, deception, addictions, compulsiveness, obsessiveness, immoral behavior, and sickness... just to name a few.

Whatever problems you are facing - whether big or small, whether you are chasing a little fox or a big one - the solution is the same: you must press in, press out and press on. You must press in to God, press out the little foxes and press on to deliverance and healing.

Giving up is not an option!

If you want deliverance, you must partner with God to exterminate the foxes from your vineyard. God is ready, willing and waiting. But we must press in, press out and press on.

Learning to Abide

1. What are some "If onlys" or "I should ofs" in your life?

2. What are your little foxes?

3. In what ways are you trying to catch your little foxes instead of allowing God to do it for you?

-11-

CALL THE HORTICULTURIST

A Healthy Vineyard

It's not enough to just rid our vineyard of the foxes. We must also repair the damage that has been done. Before our vineyard can thrive we must nurse the tender plants back to health. This can be a lengthy process of healing and mending the wounded areas of our soul. God wants to heal us so we can abide in Him.

You see, until we are healed we won't be able to abide. Our wounds will hinder us from remaining in God's presence. Our hurts will dictate our beliefs. Christa Black Gifford said it best, "If you are not anchored in the goodness of God, you will lower your theology to match your pain." Our pain will convince us God doesn't care or His Word isn't true or He can't be trusted.

Until we are healed we won't be able to abide in God's presence.

The unhealed area of our hearts is the number one hindrance to abiding. That's one of the reasons God wants to heal us: He knows until we are healed we won't be able to stay in His presence for very long.

In Matthew 9:18-34, five people came to Jesus

for healing and all five of them were healed: a 12-year old girl was raised from the dead, a woman with an issue of bleeding was cured, two blind beggars received their sight, and a demon possessed mute man was delivered and able to speak.

Five out of five were healed. You see God desires to heal all who come to Him. He is not reluctant to heal. We don't have to twist His arm behind His back. We don't have to wonder if He'll heal us. Why? Because that's the reason He came to earth. 1 John 3:8 says:

The reason the Son of God appeared was to destroy the devil's work.

Acts 10:37-38 says:

God anointed Jesus of Nazareth with the Holy Spirit and power, and how He went around doing good and healing all who were under the power of the devil, because God was with Him.

Jesus wants to heal you. He wants to heal your wounds, your hurts and your fears. He wants to heal your rejection, shame, and hopelessness. He wants to heal the vineyard of your heart so He can commune with you there.

But healing usually doesn't "just happen." Someone must do something. Yes, only Jesus can catch our foxes, but we must press in to Him and ask for our healing. The five people that were healed in Matthew 9 either did something themselves or someone else did something on their behalf.

The ruler came (on behalf of his daughter) and knelt before Jesus. The woman with the issue of bleeding came up behind Jesus and touched the edge of his cloak. The two blind beggars followed Jesus crying out for mercy. The demon possessed mute man had two friends that brought him to Jesus. Either they "came to Jesus" or someone came on their behalf.

Either way, they exercised their faith by doing what was necessary to find Jesus. They did not let anything keep them from Jesus and they did not quit until Jesus healed them.

Never Give Up

The ruler didn't quit. Even though his daughter was dead, he still pressed on. The woman with the issue of bleeding didn't quit. Even though she had to wait twelve years, then had to push through the crowds who considered her unclean, she still pressed in. The two blind beggars didn't quit. Even though Jesus passed right by them, they still pressed on. Those helping the demon possessed mute man didn't quit. Even though they were dealing with someone else's demons, they still pressed in and pressed on.

And best of all, Jesus didn't quit. When he was faced with the noisy, doubting, laughing crowds He told them to go away, He put them outside. He pressed out the crowd and raised the dead girl. He also pressed out the demons and the mute man spoke.

In all five of the healings in Matthew 9, someone pressed in, pressed out or pressed on. If we want to be healed we must do the same.

The word press means "to act on with a steady force." Not occasional force, but steady force. Not force when you feel like it, but steady force. It means to pray until we hear from God and then do what He says.

If you want to be healed, you've got to press in, press out and press on.

Deborah Oakley

| **Learning to Abide** |

1. What areas of your life need healing?

2. What are some ways you have given up?

3. How can you apply steady force to your situation?

-12-

PRESS IN, PRESS OUT AND PRESS ON

No Excuses

The things of God are not automatic. The door to Jesus is marked **PUSH**: **P**ray **U**ntil **S**omething **H**appens!

When we press in to God we press forward in our lives. Past hurts, past sins and past mistakes will try to hold us back, but we must set them aside and press in so we can press on.

You must not allow any excuse, any person, any big or little fox or any devil in hell to hold you back from seeking Jesus. You must not allow anything to keep you from getting healed and abiding in Him.

Pressing in is not easy and it is not without cost. There will be devils to defeat and obstacles to overcome. God gave the children of Israel the Promised Land, but in order to possess the land they had to press in when they felt like giving up.

When I was young I had a lot of shame. Almost every very time I had a conversation with someone I would feel an overwhelming sense of shame. I would obsess about the conversation, playing it over and over in my mind while telling myself how stupid I sounded.

Eventually, I became terrified of having conversations. So, I decided the best way to avoid this was to stay home. The technical name for this is agoraphobia, which is an irrational fear of being in public.

I really had to press in to God to conquer this. I prayed, memorized Scripture, and went to counseling. It took years to overcome, but I pressed in until I was healed.

Have you ever noticed that the longer we must wait on God the harder it is to press in? Over time we are tempted to give up. The woman with the issue of bleeding waited twelve years. She spent all her money on doctors, but was getting worse. She was unclean and the law did not allow her to touch anyone, including Jesus.

Her issue was the very thing that kept her from the only one who could heal her. She was sick and alone for twelve long years. But, that didn't stop her from pressing in to Jesus.

Many of us are just like this woman. For years we've had the same issues: anger, unforgiveness, bitterness, rejection, low self-esteem, doubt, fear and on and on. Our vineyard is a mess. It's these very issues that hinder us from pressing in to Jesus: the greatest source of power the world has ever known. Instead, we spend our time, energy and money trying to fix ourselves. We've gone to doctors, counselors, friends, family and our pastor, but we still need help. Today, Jesus is saying, "Press in to Me."

Don't let your issues keep you from the only one who can heal you.
Instead, let them be the desperation that drives you to press in to Jesus.

Maybe you feel like the woman in Matthew. She felt so unclean that she didn't dare touch Jesus. Yet, she believed that if she could just touch the hem of His garment she would be healed. And the second she did, she was healed and freed from her suffering.

Jesus didn't judge or condemn her. Instead, the Bible says He *turned towards her and saw her.* Today Jesus is turning towards you; He sees you. He sees what you are going through. No matter how rejected, cut off, or alone you feel, Jesus sees you. No matter what your issues, Jesus sees you.

Others may consider you unclean, dirty, polluted, or contaminated. Others may only see your issues, but God sees who He made you to be. And God wants to heal you.

Listen to what Jesus said in Matthew 9:22 after He healed the diseased woman, *"Take heart, daughter... your faith has healed you."* Jesus calls this sick woman "daughter." She may not have known who she was, but Jesus did. She was a child of the King.

You may not know who you are, but Jesus does. You are His child. He loves you and wants to heal you and abide with you.

Whatever our need, we must press in to Jesus. But, sometimes before we can press in we must press out. Matthew 9:32 says:

A man who was demon-possessed and could not talk was brought to Jesus. And when the demon was driven out, the man who had been mute spoke.

Jesus had to drive out the demon BEFORE the mute man could speak. Once the demon was driven out, the man was instantaneously healed. Do you feel like you are pressing in and nothing is happening? You try and try, but you can't get free.

That's because there are things in your life that are preventing you from pressing in. There are foxes hiding in your vineyard that are keeping you in bondage.

We must first press out those things that have us bound, before we can press in. Ephesians 4:22-24 says:

You were taught, with regard to your former way of life, to put off your old self, which is being corrupted by its deceitful desires; to be made new in the attitude of your minds; and to put on the new self, created to be like God in true righteousness and holiness.

We must put off before we can put on. We must put off lying and tell the truth. We must put off stealing and get a job. Before we can put on we must put off. Before we can press in we must press out.

In the early 90's, Joe and I experienced the worst years of our life. It seemed like everything was going wrong: we were struggling financially, our children were rebelling, and our church (which was our dream) failed miserably. I had a falling out with my best friend of ten years. I hated my job, I hated the house we lived in, and for the first time in our marriage my husband and I were growing apart.

So, I began to harden my heart toward God and started going my own way. Then, I met some people at work who weren't Christians. Their influence in my life wasn't good. I started drifting further and further away from God.

One day I realized what was happening. So I tried to press in to God again, but these relationships were hindering me. That's when three of my Christian friends brought me to Jesus, just like the demon-possessed mute whose friends brought him to Jesus.

They prayed over me and that was the freest I felt in a long time. But, it didn't end there. I had to drive out the ungodly relationships that were keeping me from pressing in. I had to put off and put on, press out and press in. I had to put off ungodly relationships and put on godly ones.

We see this same principle in the healing of the

ruler's daughter. When Jesus arrived at her house, He had to press out the unbelieving crowd BEFORE He could heal the girl. He told them to "Go away." It was only after they were "put outside" that the girl was healed.

We must press out whatever tries to crowd out Jesus in our lives. Maybe you need to end some ungodly relationships or quit a bad habit or stop going to certain places where you should not be going.

Don't say you are pressing in to Jesus if you're unwilling to press out some things in your life!

Some of us allow a busy schedule to crowd Jesus out. "Well, I'm just too busy to pray or read God's word." No, you're not. It's just not your priority. You make time for what's important to you.

We must press out whatever tries to crowd out Jesus in our lives. Then we can press in and lastly... we can press on.

In Matthew 9:27, we read about two blind men who followed Jesus seeking healing. Think about that: it can't be easy to follow someone when you can't see!

Although they were crying out for mercy, Jesus ignored them. He took off for the home of Jairus leaving these blind men behind. He just kept on going as though they weren't even there.

When they arrived at the house of Jairus, Jesus left them outside and went into the house of Jairus to heal his daughter. Talk about having to press on. Then, they still had to follow Jesus into the house where He finally healed them.

Then, there's Jairus the ruler. When he left his daughter to find Jesus she was alive. On the journey, Jairus finds out she's dead. He could have given up right then, but he kept pressing on. If we want healing we must press in, press out and press on.

Say Goodbye To The Little Foxes

There will be times when you need strength from God, so you press in. There will be times you need a word from God, so you press in. There will be times you need help from God, so you press in.

When the enemy tries to hold you back, you press him out! When your past tries to hold you back, you press it out! When fear of failure tries to hold you back, you press it out!

There will be hindrances to overcome, but you press on! There will be difficult circumstances, but you press on! You may fall, but you get back up and press on! You may fail, but you learn from it and press on!

There will be times you think you should quit, but you press on! There will be times others think you should quit, but you press on! There will be times you feel like you'll never make it, but you press on!

Do you want physical, emotional and spiritual healing? Do you want to touch the hem of His garment? Do you want resurrection life? Do you want to see again? Do you want deliverance? Do you want to abide in the presence of God?

Then, press in and never let anything keep you from pressing in! Press out and never let anything keep you from pressing out! Press on and never let anything keep you from pressing on!

Say goodbye to the little foxes. Say so long to the big foxes. Let Jesus empower you to take back your vineyard. Let Him heal you. He is the Vine and you are the branches. Apart from Him you can do nothing, but with Him there's nothing you cannot do!

Abide

| **Learning to Abide** |

1. How can you press in?

2. What do you need to press out in your life?

3. What excuses are using that are keeping you from pressing in or pressing on?

4. Are your friends influencing your life for good by bringing you closer to Jesus?

5. What ungodly relationships do you need to end?

6. What bad habit do you need to stop?

7. What places should you not be going?

Abide

SECTION FOUR

THE BENEFITS OF ABIDING IN CHRIST

Abide

-13-
YOU DON'T HAVE TO SETTLE

Cheese And Crackers

Years ago, before transatlantic flight was common, a man wanted to travel from the United States to Europe. He worked hard and saved until he had just enough money to purchase a ticket on a ship. Then he filled a suitcase with enough cheese and crackers to last him on the three-week journey. That was all he could afford. Every meal, when all the other passengers would go to the ornate dining room to eat their gourmet food, this man would go to a corner of the ship so no one could see him and eat his cheese and crackers. This went on day after day.

As he would eat his cheese and crackers, he could smell the delicious food being served in the dining room. After dinner, the other passengers would talk about how good the food was. They would rub their bellies and complain about how full they were and how they would have to go on a diet after the trip. The poor traveler wanted to join the other passengers, but he had no extra money. Sometimes, he would lie awake at night dreaming of the scrumptious food.

As the trip was coming to an end, one of the passengers approached him and said, "Sir, I can't help but notice that you are always over there eating those cheese and crackers at mealtimes. Why don't you come into the banquet hall and eat with us?" Feeling embarrassed the traveler replied, "Well, to tell you the truth, I only had enough money to buy a ticket. I don't have any extra money to buy meals." The other passenger raised his eyebrows in surprise. He shook his head and said, "Sir, don't you realize the meals are included in the price of the ticket? Your meals have already been paid for."

Many of us are just like this traveler. God has prepared a banquet for us, but we sit in the corner eating cheese and crackers. We are missing out on God's best because we don't realize the good things in life have already been paid for since we are "Abiding In Christ."

Remember, "in Christ" we are royalty, saints and heirs. We have all spiritual blessings.

We don't have to settle for cheese and crackers. You see, every time we go around in fear and anxiety, we are eating cheese and crackers. Every time we doubt the promises of God for our life we are eating cheese and crackers. Every time we settle for less than God's best we are choosing cheese and crackers. A place has already been set for us at the banquet table and the price has already been paid. There are benefits for those who abide in Christ.

My husband and I settled for cheese and

crackers for way too many years. We mistakenly bought into the lie that if you were a Christian minister or pastor you should be poor. We erroneously and unconsciously believed that the less we had financially the more pleasing we were to God. Sacrifice was the operative word. Anything else could be seen as greed or selfishness.

So, we were underpaid and overworked most of the time. After a long and sometimes difficult day at the office we would come home and agonize over how to pay the bills. Vacations were few and far between due to lack of funds. Money was always tight. For two decades we lived under the weight of this self-imposed poverty.

If someone tried to bless us financially we would feel guilty if we accepted their generosity. It made us uncomfortable. We would say things like, "Oh, that's okay," meaning you shouldn't waste your time or money on us. Or we'd try to talk them out of blessing us by saying, "Are you sure? You don't have to do that."

After all this, if for some unforeseen reason they still wanted to bless us, we would reluctantly accept... secretly rejoicing in the unexpected gift. God had set a banquet table for us and we kept trying to eat cheese and crackers.

Take Your Seat At The Table

Today, Joe and I no longer settle for cheese and

crackers. We are feasting at God's banquet table of abundance, not just financially, but in every area of our lives. We enjoy good health. We live in our dream house. We have a dream job pastoring Grace Fellowship Church. Our church is financially stable. We have friends that love us. We get to travel all over the world. Our children are serving God and prosperous. Our grandchildren are healthy, happy and in church. Our lives are overflowing with fruitfulness.

Deuteronomy 28:3-6 pretty much sums up our lives:

You will be blessed in the city and blessed in the country. The fruit of your womb will be blessed, and the crops of your land and the young of your livestock — the calves of your herds and the lambs of your flocks. Your basket and your kneading trough will be blessed. You will be blessed when you come in and blessed when you go out.

This is how we want to live our lives. This is how God wants us to live our lives. He doesn't want us to live in poverty and lack, but in abundance and prosperity.

When we abide, dwell, live, and make our abode in God, blessing is the only natural outcome.

When we abide in Christ, fruitfulness is unavoidable. It is the earmark of abiding in Christ.

So, let's look at five benefits of abiding in God's presence. Be assured there are many more than five. If you filled the annals of every library in the world you would never exhaust the benefits of a life lived in God's presence. This is just a starting place. God's banquet table is set. So pull up a chair, have a seat, and dig in.

Abide

Learning to Abide

1. How have you settled for "cheese and crackers" in your life?

2. What is one area that you are believing God for abundance in your life?

-14-

THE BENEFIT OF FRUITFULNESS

The first benefit I want to talk about is this: abiding produces fruitfulness. Jesus said in John 15:4-5:

Abide in Me, and I in you. As the branch cannot bear fruit of itself, unless it abides in the vine, neither can you, unless you abide in Me. I am the Vine, you are the branches. He who abides in Me, and I in him, bears much fruit; for without Me you can do nothing.

It is unarguably clear that fruitfulness is the outcome of abiding. To be fruitful means to bear fruit and to grow and increase. Galatians 5:22-23 describes this fruit.

But the fruit of the Spirit is love, joy, peace, patience, kindness, goodness, faithfulness, gentleness and self-control.

Are these fruit being produced in your life?

Life has a way of squeezing us, and when we are squeezed, our fruit is either sweet or bitter.

What comes out of you when the squeeze is on? That's how you know what fruit you're producing. You see, it's easy to be kind when someone is kind to us. But what do you do when someone is mean or rude? Are you mean or rude back? What happens when someone hurts you? Do you hurt them back?

What happens when life gets hard... really hard? You know, those times when nothing seems to be going your way, those times when you feel alone, those times when it seems like no one cares.

What happens when your dreams don't turn out the way you thought they would? When the pressure is on, do you still produce the fruit of the spirit? Do you love those who hate you? Do you have joy in the midst of despairing circumstances? Do you have peace when you're surrounded by turmoil? If not, then you are not abiding. You are trying to produce fruit with your own self-effort and strength. However, that's not how fruit is produced.

A Lesson From An Orange Tree

I remember a time when my husband and I were biking through an orange grove in Florida. We didn't hear the orange trees huffing and puffing, grunting and groaning, as they tried to produce oranges. The oranges were not produced by self-effort; they were a by-product of the life that was in the tree.

When we are abiding in Christ the fruit grows naturally. It's a by-product of worshiping, being in the Word and prayer. We don't have to work at it. We don't have to agonize over it. We don't have to struggle to produce fruit. You see:

We can't conform ourselves to His image.
We can't produce Christ-like character.
We can't work up fruit on our own.

The Holy Spirit produces the fruit of the spirit. The life-sap of the Holy Spirit is the only way to grow spiritual fruit. A branch naturally has the same DNA as the trunk. God created us in His image. Therefore, His DNA is our DNA (Genesis 1:26-27). If God's DNA is love, then our DNA will be love. If God's DNA is self-control, then our DNA will be self-control. If God's DNA is peace, then our DNA will be peace.

Fruitfulness is a benefit of abiding in God.
Change happens when we abide in God.
Things get better when we abide in God.

If you're relying on yourself to change things you're really in trouble. You can't produce fruit in your life apart from God (John 15:5). You need Him. This means you run to Him with your troubles. You trust Him, believe Him, and rely on Him to turn things around. I think most of us try to rely on self-effort and will power. But we need less will power and more of God's power!

The New Math

We can't change our self with more of self because all we're doing is trying to increase our self. More of self does not result in less of self.

Abide

More of the flesh doesn't result in less of the flesh. The ability to live and love like Jesus doesn't happen by addition only. We can't just ADD Christ-like character to our lives. The ability to live and love like Jesus also happens in subtraction. It's less of me and more of Him. I must decrease and He must increase.

Often we think, "If I just try harder I can change myself." But, the harder we try the more we fail. We can't just will ourselves to produce fruit. That's why the Bible calls it the "fruit of the Spirit." It's not the fruit of the flesh. Scripture is painfully clear that within myself there is nothing good. Philippians 3:3 says:

For it is we who are the circumcision, we who worship by the Spirit of God, who glory in Christ Jesus, and who put no confidence in the flesh...

Romans 7:18 says:

For I know that nothing good lives in me, that is in my sinful nature.

If I want to produce good fruit I must surrender to the Spirit of God, quit trying to change myself in my own strength and allow the Holy Spirit to live and love through me.

I remember when my husband and I started Grace Fellowship Church. Everyone was so excited to be a part of what God was doing. I had so much love for the people that came to our church. Joe and I felt so loved and supported. It was so easy to love them back.

But as time went on, some of these same people stopped being loving and supportive. As a matter of fact, they were anything but loving and supportive. Instead, they became angry and at times really mean. At this point it wasn't hard for me to love them... it was impossible. I felt hurt and betrayed. So, I started trying harder. But, the harder I tried the more I failed.

Finally, it hit me one day: I just can't do this. My love isn't enough. My love is falling short. My love is conditional. This was a big wake up call for me. I remember standing in the foyer of my house telling God, "I just can't love people the way I should." I remember as clear as day God said to me, "No, you can't, but I can love them through you." I knew in that instant that I had to die to the belief that "I" could love others in my own strength. So, I cried out to God for an impartation of His love into my heart and He gave it to me.

I wish I could say that since then I've never struggled with loving people. I can't say that. But, I can say that since that day I've realized that I can't love people without God's help. I am totally, completely, and entirely dependent on God's love in order to give love. I can't do it my way. My way is fruitless.

"I" had to get out of the way for Jesus to have His way. "I" had to admit my helplessness and rely on God's faithfulness.

I had tried to obey God's command to love. However, it was a self-driven effort to conform my behavior without God changing my heart. But, outward conformity to legalistic rules won't cut it. I had to die to self-effort and depend on God. I had to abide in Christ in order to love those who didn't love me. When I finally realized this, I began to see fruit in my life. I was beginning to understand the benefits of abiding in Christ.

Gifts And Fruit – You Need Both

Unfortunately, many people emphasize the gifts of the Spirit and neglect the fruit of the Spirit. However, both are necessary. The difference between them is this: gifts are given; fruit is grown. The gifts of the Spirit are manifestations of God's power; the fruit of the Spirit are manifestations of God's character.

The gifts of the Spirit show what God does. The fruit of the Spirit show who God is.

Our part is to receive the gifts of the Spirit and grow the fruit in the power of the Spirit. When we abide in Christ we grow fruit and become more like Christ.

Our spouses need us to be Christ-like. Our children need Christ-like parents. Our friends need Christ-like examples. So, how is this fruit produced in our lives? Is it by man's effort? Not at all. Just as the branch derives life from the vine, so the believer in Christ derives his life from the True Vine in order to bear fruit.

Fruit In The Valley

Remember, life can be difficult even if you're a Christian. Being a Christian doesn't exempt us from the troubles of life. Psalms 34:19 says:

A righteous man may have many troubles, but the Lord delivers him from them all.

Fortunately, this passage promises deliverance, but it doesn't promise a trouble-free life. As Christians we will have mountains to cross and valleys to forge. We will have good days and bad days. We will have times of joy and times of despair, times of plenty and times of lack, times of success and times of failure. But, here's the key to our fruitfulness in these valleys: abiding in Christ.

When we abide in Him, God will turn our trials into our greatest blessings. Even our worst moments will produce a fruitful harvest. How would you like that?

Think about the worst thing you've ever gone through. Now imagine God using it for good. Imagine Him bringing healing out of hurt and freedom out of captivity. Imagine a fresh start without the regrets of the past. God can produce a fruitful harvest out of your troubles. That's what He can do if you abide in Him.

Isaiah 61:1-3 says:

Abide

The Spirit of the Sovereign Lord is on me, because the Lord has anointed me to preach the good news to the poor. He sent me to bind up the brokenhearted, to proclaim freedom for the captives and release from darkness for the prisoners, to proclaim the year of the Lord's favor and the day of vengeance of our God, to comfort all who mourn, and provide for those who grieve in Zion. To bestow on them a crown of beauty instead of ashes, the oil of gladness instead of mourning, and a garment of praise instead of a spirit of despair.

Isaiah declared all this to be possible because *the Spirit of the Lord was upon Him.* You could say this is the Old Testament equivalent of abiding. Since Christ had not yet been crucified, Old Testament believers didn't have the Holy Spirit indwelling them. Instead the Holy Spirit would *come upon them* to empower and enable them to be fruitful. As they yielded to the Spirit of God, He would enable them to be fruitful. Likewise, as we yield to the Spirit of God, He enables us to be fruitful.

Learning to Abide

1. In what ways are you relying on yourself to produce fruitfulness?

2. What areas do you need to surrender to God?

-15-
THE BENEFIT OF PRUNING

Ouch! That Hurts!

The first benefit of abiding in Christ is fruitfulness. The second benefit of abiding is pruning.

You're probably thinking, "WHAT? I thought we were talking about benefits. Pruning doesn't sound like a benefit." But it is. Here's why. In John 15:1-2, Jesus said:

I am the true vine, and My Father is the vinedresser. Every branch in Me that does not bear fruit He takes away; and every branch that bears fruit He prunes, that it may bear more fruit.

Pruning is a benefit of abiding because it produces more fruit. Remember, fruit is having godly characteristics and character in our lives, and that requires pruning.

Now, I'm sure if the branches could talk, they would tell you that pruning is painful. As a matter of fact, if you want to know the areas that God is pruning in your life, ask yourself, "Where am I hurting?" The places of pain are where His pruning shears are cutting something away.

God will cut away everything in our lives that interferes with our relationship with Him.

Yes, pruning hurts, but it also helps. We may not enjoy it, but we need it. The painful season of pruning is inevitable, but so is the resulting fruitfulness. Actually, I would be more afraid of God NOT pruning me than the pain of being pruned.

Call The Exterminator

The Bible Exposition Commentary describes how unattended vines left to themselves will grow wild. They will produce huge canopies that hinder fruitfulness. This makes them susceptible to disease, bugs and insects. As a matter of fact, according to the *Strong's Concordance* the Greek word for prune is "cleanse."

Pruning cleanses us from spiritual disease, bugs and insects in our soul.

Pruning also involves cutting away the good fruit in order to produce the best fruit.

Sometimes this means cutting away whole clusters of grapes so that the rest of the vine will yield a better quality harvest. This can seem counter-productive, but it isn't.

Pruning can turn a beautiful, plentiful vine into a not-so-attractive looking plant. But, there is a purpose for this. Grapevines can become so dense that the sun cannot penetrate the areas where more fruit should grow. These unnurtured areas usually shrivel, wilt and eventually die.

Sometimes God must cut things out of our lives that "seem good" so that the SON can reach into other areas of our lives that aren't producing fruit.

Are there areas in your life that aren't bearing fruit? Instead of trying to fix yourself, will you allow God to prune you? Will you invite the Holy Spirit to cut away the unfruitful areas in your soul? It may seem painful at first, but in the end your life will be so much more fruitful.

Another part of pruning involves removing suckers. A sucker is a very small branch that grows in the fork of the main trunk of the tree. It saps the life from the fruit-producing branches.

Suckers might be those people or situations in our lives that just suck the life out of us. Maybe it's a friend that drains you with their negativity, gossip, or lack of faith. Maybe it's a situation that tempts you to sin. Perhaps you are going to places you have no business going to.

God must cut these things out of our lives so we can bear more fruit. That's what pruning means. It means to cut away that which is unnecessary or unwanted to encourage fuller growth. So, do you see why pruning is a benefit?

Actually, pruning is the most important part of the whole vineyard. The people who prune must be wisely trained. It can take three years to learn how to properly prune. It is a process that requires precision and skill and must be executed with tender, loving care.

John 15:1 says that the Father is the Vinedresser. A vinedresser is the keeper of the vineyard. His pruning is exact. He has one goal: fruitfulness. And that requires pruning.

**God is never nearer to you
than when He is pruning you.**

God is pruning you for your good. Pruning is not a punishment. In fact, it's a process designed to make you look more like Christ.

One of the most skillfully pruned landscapes in the U.S. is at Disney World in Orlando, Florida. I love how the hedges are pruned to look like Disney characters such as Mickey Mouse and Donald Duck. These hedges didn't just grow to reflect these Disney characters. Someone had to prune them. They had to cut off any branches that didn't look like Mickey or Donald. They had to shape these bushes into the image of these Disney characters.

In much the same way, God prunes us to shape us into the image of Jesus. Sometimes the pruning involves cutting away sin, distractions, misbeliefs, bad influences or bad attitudes from our lives.

**Yes, pruning is painful, but God is changing
us to look more like Jesus.**

Abide

The more we abide in Christ, the more fruit we bear; and the more fruit we bear, the more we need to be pruned.

No Fruit, Fruit, More Fruit And Much Fruit

Did you know there are degrees of fruitfulness? Actually, John 15 describes four degrees of fruitfulness: no fruit, fruit, more fruit, and much fruit. The question is – which one are you? Are you willing to be pruned so you can bear more fruit?

Learning to Abide

1. What are some painful areas in your life?

2. What are some situations that need to be pruned away in your life?

3. Are you producing no fruit, fruit, more fruit, or much fruit?

-16-
THE BENEFIT OF LOVE

So far we've seen that two benefits of abiding in Christ are fruitfulness and pruning. The third benefit of abiding in Christ is love. Portions of 1 John 4:12-15 say:

If we love one another, God abides in us, and His love has been perfected in us. By this we know that we abide in Him, and He in us, because He has given us of His Spirit. Whoever confesses that Jesus is the Son of God, God abides in Him, and he in God. God is love, and he who abides in love abides in God, and God in him.

If You Have God You Have Love

Here's the bottom line: abiding is made possible by the indwelling of the Holy Spirit. If you are a born again believer, then God lives in you and you live in God.

Since God is love, you have love living on the inside of you.

1 John 4:16 says:

And we have known and believed the love that God has for us.

Notice it says we have "known and believed." Some of us know God loves us, but we don't really believe it. We might believe God will do it for others, but we really don't believe He will do it for us; not after the things we've done, not after the mess we've made. Isaiah 49:13-16 says:

Shout for joy, O heavens; rejoice, O earth; burst into song, O mountains! For the Lord comforts His people and will have compassion on His afflicted ones. But Zion said, "The Lord has forsaken me, the Lord has forgotten me." "Can a mother forget the baby at her breast and have no compassion on the child she has borne? Though she may forget, I will not forget you! See, I have engraved you on the palms of my hands; your walls are ever before me."

Most of the time we see God as Father, which is right and good. But here we see that God loves like a mother. Here's the thing about a mother's love... mothers love their children no matter what they've done. That's how God loves us. No matter what we've done He loves us and He's there for us. He will not forget us or forsake us. His love is compassionate and comforting.

Unending Love

This passage also says "our walls" are ever before Him. This is literally speaking of the walls of Jerusalem – which at that very moment were torn down. The city was in ruins and the people were dispersed due to their sin. Yet God says to them, "I'll never forget you. I think about you all the time. Even though you've made a huge mess of things, I still love you!"

God says the same thing to us: "I'll never forget you. I'll never give up on you. No matter what, I still love you. You've made a mess, I still love you! You've fallen down, I still love you! You aren't sure you love Me? I STILL LOVE YOU! That will never change!" Get this down in your spirit today. Such is the love of God.

Nothing can make God stop loving you!

You see, God's love is for you. This message is not for someone else. It's for you. Your deepest need is the love of God. It doesn't matter who you are – God loves you. It doesn't matter what you've done – God loves you. This is how God loves us. This is how we are to love others.

Our ability to love others is in direct proportion to how much we receive God's love for us.

Jesus did not simply preach the love of God; He proved His love by giving His life on the cross. He showed His love by His actions. He expects us to do the same. If we abide in His love, we must share this love with others. Think about it: the branches do not eat the fruit; others eat it. We are not producing fruit to feed ourselves, but to serve others. Proverbs 10:21 says:

The lips of the righteous feed many.

Here's the astounding thing: the world will not believe that God loves them until they see His love in us (John 13:34-35). When Jesus was on the earth He revealed God to the world. But, Jesus is no longer here on the earth. How then, does God reveal Himself to the world? Through us! Men cannot see God, but they can see us. They will believe in God when they see us loving one another. Galatians 5:6 says:

The only thing that counts is faith expressing itself through love.

When we understand this it will impact every aspect of our Christian walk. When we don't understand this it will hinder every aspect of our Christian walk. It will hinder:

- Our faith - How can we believe God to change us if we don't even believe He loves us?
- Our worship - How can we praise someone who doesn't love us?
- Our love for ourselves - If God doesn't love us, how can we love us?
- Our love for others - If God doesn't love us, how can we love others?

You see, nothing is going to change our hearts except love. Proverbs 19:22 says:

What a man desires is unfailing love.

The second we stop loving is the second we stop abiding. God is love and if we cease to love we cease to abide. But, if we abide we have the benefit of being able to love even the unlovely.

Abide

Learning to Abide

1. Are there areas in your life where you feel God does not love you?

2. In what areas of your life are you relying on willpower?

3. In what areas of your life do you feel alone?

-17-
THE BENEFIT OF FREEDOM

The fourth benefit of abiding is that it produces freedom in our lives. John 8:31-32 says:

If you abide in My word, you are My disciples indeed. And you shall know the truth, and the truth shall make you free.

Most people believe that freedom follows a power encounter with the enemy, but most of the time it actually follows a truth encounter. Yes, we must take authority over our enemy in Jesus' name, but we overcome Satan the same way Jesus did: by speaking the truth of God's Word.

Words are the enemy's main tool. Think about it – his tactics include temptation, accusation, condemnation, and deception – all words. Think about the way Goliath had discouraged the army of Israel from fighting before David defeated him. He had beaten the Israelites without a single action, only through his words.

Since the enemy's main tool is deception, we must operate in the opposite spirit, which is truth. That's why truth sets us free! And truth requires abiding in God's Word. You will never be free apart from abiding. You will never conquer your enemies apart from abiding. You will never live a victorious Christian life apart from abiding.

Let Freedom Ring

Christianity without abiding is like a car without an engine. Christianity without abiding is like a train without tracks. Christianity without abiding is like a house without a foundation. Without an engine a car has no power. Without tracks a train has no direction. Without a foundation a house has no stability.

Without abiding in Christ our Christian life will have no power, no direction, no stability and no freedom.

2 Corinthians 3:17 says:

Now the Lord is the Spirit, and where the Spirit of the Lord is, there is freedom.

We see here that freedom is found "where the Spirit of the Lord is." So, we must be where the Spirit is. That's how we get free: by abiding where the Spirit abides. You see, abiding in God's Spirit can bring life out of death. It can bring healing out of hurt. It can bring hope out of despair. It can bring joy out of sorrow. It can bring power out of weakness. Zechariah 4:6 tells us it's:

'Not by might nor by power, but by My Spirit,' says the Lord Almighty.

No matter how bound up you are, the Spirit of God can free you. No matter how hurt you are, the Spirit of God can heal you. No matter how down you are, the Spirit of God can lift you. No matter how dry you are, the Spirit can refresh you. No matter how empty you are, the Spirit of God can fill you. That's the key – being filled with the Spirit of God, and that requires abiding in God.

What Is Your Alcatraz?

According to the *Encarta Dictionary,* one of the definitions of freedom is "release or rescue from being physically bound, or from being confined, enslaved, captured, or imprisoned." Although most of us will never be physically bound, many of us are spiritually bound, enslaved, confined and imprisoned. We live our lives controlled by sin and under the influence of Satan and our flesh.

Recently my husband and I went to San Francisco, California. While we were there we did a tour of Alcatraz Federal Penitentiary. Alcatraz was a maximum high-security prison from 1933 until 1963. The 1,576 prisoners that did time on Alcatraz lived in a 9' by 5' by 7' high primitive cell. They were given a cot, a sink, a toilet, a desk, a pillow and a blanket. Inmates were given food, clothing, shelter and medical attention. Anything else was considered a privilege.

Up until the late 1930's Alcatraz had a rule of silence. Inmates were not allowed to talk to one another except at meal time and recreation periods. This was another form of imprisonment

Abide

in itself. Prisoners were only allowed to go outside on Saturdays, Sundays and holidays for a maximum of five hours. Prisoners who went to the isolation cells were treated inhumanely.

Living life imprisoned on Alcatraz was no picnic. It was a hard life void of freedom and comfort. Many prisoners compared it to living in hell.

Sad to say, many Christians live their lives in a spiritual Alcatraz. We forfeit our freedom and privileges as children of God and live like prisoners; we live bound by sin, we're enslaved by addictions, we're defeated in our relationships, our marriages are falling apart, we have mountains of debt, we feel hopeless, afraid and discouraged.

One of my prisons has been discouragement. As a pastor and preacher I encountered a lot of rejection and judgment for being a woman in these roles. As a result I became extremely discouraged. I wanted so much for others to accept and acknowledge my calling. When they didn't I would spiral downward into a deep place of discouragement and despair. I would begin to doubt my calling and doubt God's will for my life. As a result I would lose my confidence. I was so bound by what others thought of me that I lived in the pit of discouragement for years.

It was only when I began to care more about what Jesus thought than what others thought that I started getting free. When I would feel rejected I would quote verses like Ephesians 1:6:

To the praise of the glory of His grace, wherein He hath made us accepted in the beloved.

I stood on His Word and sought Him in prayer. I trusted Him to give me strength and to set me free. I fought discouragement by getting in the Word and getting the Word in me. I clung to Jesus like a life-preserver because He was preserving my life. I chose to abide in Jesus and as a result He set me free.

Listen to what Jesus says in Luke 4:18-19:

"The Spirit of the Lord is on me, because He has anointed me to preach good news to the poor. He has sent me to proclaim freedom for the prisoners and recovery of sight for the blind, to release the oppressed, to proclaim the year of the Lord's favor."

Jesus came to proclaim freedom for the prisoners. Satan wants to keep us bound, but Jesus brings us good news. We're free. He has unlocked our prison door and released us from every chain that has kept us bound. We don't deserve it and we can't earn it. But God made a way for us to be free.

In John 14:6-7 Jesus said:

"I am the way and the truth and the life. No one comes to the Father except through Me."

On our own we would rot away in prison, but Jesus came to make a way out for us. Now it's

Abide

up to us to choose Him. That means we abide with Him. There is no other way. There is only one way. He is the only way. But we have to choose Him.

So Close Yet So Far

Alcatraz was built on an island made of rock in the San Francisco Bay. It is located one-and a-half miles off the shore of San Francisco. When prisoners were allowed outdoors they could look across the bay and see the city of San Francisco in the distance. Some could see it from their prison cells.

This beautiful city was only a painful reminder of what they would never have. They would never be free to walk the streets or stand on Fisherman's Wharf or ride a cable car or dine in China Town. All they could do was gaze across the Bay and dream of being free. Freedom was so close yet so far.

Many Christians live their lives just like this; imprisoned, gazing at their unfulfilled dreams, longing for freedom but it never comes. They spend their lives wishing, hoping, longing but never achieving their dreams.

Abiding in Jesus is the only way to freedom.

Nothing you do apart from abiding in Him is ever going to bring real, lasting freedom. Will you make it your life endeavor to seek to abide? If you do, you will be free.

Learning to Abide

1. What are some areas where you feel imprisoned in life?

2. What lies are you believing that keep you bound up?

3. What truth from God's Word will you apply to your situation?

-18-

THE BENEFIT OF OBEDIENCE

The fifth benefit of abiding is that it results in obedience in our lives. 1 John 3:24 says:

Now he who keeps His commandments abides in Him, and He in him.

The instant we ask Jesus into our heart He comes to live in us and commune with us. Maintaining that communion requires a moment-by-moment obedience. When we disobey it separates us from God's presence. So, to abide in God's presence we *must be* obedient. We also must abide in God's presence *to be* obedient.

The secret to obedience is not willpower – but submitting your will to His power!

Will Power Versus His Power

Obedience to God is not about willpower. Obedience is not about being a "self-made" man or woman, but being God-made! It's natural to try to change ourselves by sheer willpower alone, but eventually we see the painful truth that we are powerless. We discover our inability to add one single inch to our spiritual stature. All our attempts to fix ourselves will end in defeat. Our good intentions will fail. Even our efforts to be good will come up short.

That's what Paul was talking about in Romans 7:15-25 when he said:

For what I am doing, I do not understand. For what I will to do, that I do not practice; but what I hate, that I do. If, then, I do what I will not to do, I agree with the law that it is good. But now, it is no longer I who do it, but sin that dwells in me. For I know that in me (that is, in my flesh) nothing good dwells; for to will is present with me, but how to perform what is good I do not find... Now if I do what I will not to do, it is no longer I who do it, but sin that dwells in me. O wretched man that I am! Who will deliver me from this body of death? I thank God — through Jesus Christ our Lord!

When I was first saved I was very addicted to cigarettes. I smoked two or three packs a day. I was determined to quit. I was sure I could do it. I was totally confident in myself to give up cigarettes, but nothing I did worked.

You see, I had the will to do good, but I couldn't figure out how. I tried so hard, but I couldn't even go one hour without a cigarette. I was determined, but I was powerless over nicotine. My will was surrendered to God, I wanted to do the right thing, but I always ended up doing it wrong. You see, God was teaching me that will power alone isn't enough. What I needed was His power.

I had will power, but I hadn't submitted my will to His power.

So, I cried out to God. I confessed my sin and powerlessness and asked God to give me His power. I was acknowledging that He was the Vine and I was just the branch. I was like a helpless grape just hanging there waiting for His life and power to flow through me. From that day till now I've never picked up another cigarette. Why? Because I gave up on self-effort and asked God for His power to change me. Paul says it best in Philippians 2:13:

For it is God who works in you to will and to act according to His good purpose.

Because the branch is the direct counterpart of the Vine, we can do nothing without Him. If we want to live in obedience and bring forth fruit, we must realize this: we cannot live in obedience apart from abiding in Jesus. There is nothing good in us apart from abiding in Christ. All our righteousness is as filthy rags (Isaiah 64:6). We are beggars at the table of God's mercy. We are unworthy, unfaithful and undeserving. But, glory to God... when we are weak, He is strong. When we are unrighteous, He is our righteousness. When we mess up, He picks us up.

He Carries You

I've heard people say that Christians are weak people who use God as a crutch. I want to tell them, "He's not a crutch; He's a stretcher." When I fall He picks me up and carries me. Apart from Him, I don't even have the strength to limp! And when I want to do things my way, when my will is weak, when I can't resist temptation, when I can't control my mouth, when I don't want to read my Bible or be kind to someone who is being ugly to me or when I want to go places I know I shouldn't, I run to Him... I reconnect to Jesus my Vine. He's the Vine that provides the strength, the sap and the life that I need. I'm the branch that just hangs there helplessly waiting to receive.

Beloved, a deep conviction of this truth lies at the very root of your obedience:

Apart from Him you can do nothing!

Another way to say this is: apart from Him you can to "no thing". I'm not saying we don't have any part in all this. We do. There's man's responsibility and God's sovereignty. Yes, we must choose God's will, but we must realize that even the decision to choose God's will is from God. He works in us - helping us to want to obey Him - and then helping us do what He wants. If it weren't for God we couldn't even choose to do His will. Paul puts it this way in 2 Corinthians 12:9-10:

My grace is sufficient for you, for My power is made perfect in weakness. Therefore I will boast all the more gladly about my weaknesses, so that Christ's power may rest on me. That is why, for Christ's sake, I delight in weaknesses... For when I am weak, then I am strong.

Today, I submit to you that we are all weak.

Abide

We have hope, but we get discouraged.
We believe, but we doubt.
We have faith, but we still fear.
We love and we hate.
We pray and we don't pray.
We obey and we disobey.

But one truth remains the same: apart from Him we can do nothing. But through Him we can do all things. The benefits of abiding in Christ are fruitfulness, pruning, love, freedom and obedience.

He Is Always With You

Here's the best benefit of all: we are never alone. No matter what happens in life, we are never alone. No matter how hard life is, we are never alone. On a good day or a bad day, we are never alone. When we abide in the True Vine, God is always with us. We may not see Him or feel Him, but God is always with us. He is in us and His Spirit follows us and watches over us and protects us, and helps us. He is Emmanuel... God with us.

Dr. Tony Campolo tells the story of when he was a boy growing up in a congested and busy city. His mother was concerned for his wellbeing, so she arranged for a teenage girl who lived nearby to walk home with him from school. She paid her a nickel a day. But, Tony rebelled in the second grade and told his mother, "I'll walk myself to school and if you give me a nickel a week, I'll be extra careful. You can keep the rest of the money and we'll both be better off."

After a period of pleading and begging, little Tony finally got his way. For the next two years he walked eight blocks back and forth to school. He was careful and didn't talk to strangers along the way.

Years later at a family party, Tony began bragging about how independent he was as a child walking to school all by himself. His mother just laughed and then finished the rest of the story. "Did you really think you were alone?" she asked. "Every morning when you left for school, I left with you. I walked behind you all the way. You never saw me, but I was there following you every step of the way."

How many of us are just like Tony Campolo? In our everyday walk through life we think we are alone. We think we are doing it on our own. We're so focused on where we're going and how "we're" going to get there that we fail to recognize that God is with us every step of the way. We fail to recognize that He is watching over us like a mother watches over the child she loves.

God is always with us. He faithfully watches over us and we are never alone. He is Emmanuel, God with us. He is the True Vine and He abides in us and we abide in Him.

Abide

| **Learning to Abide** |

1. Are you living life by will-power or by submitting your will to His power?

2. What are some areas in your life that you are being obedient to God?

3. What are some areas in your life that you are not being obedient to God?

4. What is keeping you from being obedient?

5. Are you aware of God's presence in your life on a daily basis?

6. What can you do to cultivate that awareness of God's presence?

Abide

Deborah Oakley

EPILOGUE

Abide

Have you ever heard a sermon, watched a movie or read a book where they saved the best for last? I hope that is what I have done. I hope I've saved the best for last. Not that anything can top abiding in God. It can't. But, what I have to share is connected to abiding. It's one more element of how to abide.

At the beginning of this book I gave you a thorough definition of the word abide. Well, almost thorough. In case you forgot, let's review it:

Abide means:
To stay in a certain place.
The abode where we live.
To continue, dwell, endure and remain.
To remain stable and to stand fast.

But, that's not all it means. I purposely left out one critical part of the definition. So here it is:

Abide also means:
To stay in a given place, state, relation or expectancy; to wait on and to expect.

Did you catch the added part? It's the part about expectancy. Wow! Do you realize what this means? Our earlier definition dealt with the question of "where?" Where do we live? Where do we dwell? Where do we remain? The answer of course is with God.

This later definition deals with the question of "how long?" How long must I wait to get to this place and then how long must I wait once I'm there? The answer of course is as long as it takes.

Wow again! In order to abide in Christ we must have an expectancy that we will abide. We must have faith and believe that no matter how long it takes, the end result is the same: we will abide in Christ.

It also means that once we abide we fully expect to continue in the place of abiding. We don't just pop in and out of God's presence. Abiding isn't a casual visit; it's an intentional lifelong lingering. The expectation is to stay there, to make our abode there.

Of course, it also means that we live a life of expectancy, specifically when our expectations are delayed. That means we have faith, hope and anticipation even if it seems like our prayers aren't answered. We believe that God is for us and has good things in store for us. We believe that God's dwelling place is overflowing with blessings, favor, goodness, answered prayer, healing, provision, victory, and whatever else we need. This is our expectation, no matter how long we have to wait for it. No matter what happens we will abide with God and expect good things in our life.

So let's get practical. What does this mean for us on a day-to-day basis?

Let me give you an example from my own life.

Deborah Oakley

Ten years ago my husband and I received a word from God that He wanted our church to be landowners, not renters. We were renting a building that was falling apart. We were paying a lot of money in rent and we felt God wanted us to build our own equity not someone else's. We also believed our legacy required a permanent dwelling place. We believed God was telling us to either buy land and build or find an already pre-existing building and purchase it for our church.

"Great," we thought. That sounded like a good plan; except we didn't have any money. What we had was a lot of faith. If God wanted us to own land and a building, He would provide.

During this time, my husband heard about a program that Hobby Lobby had that helped churches buy buildings. So, for two long and sometimes frustrating years he went through all the necessary steps to qualify our church for this program. It was a happy day when we found out we were accepted. Now we could begin our search.

First, we considered buying an existing building in a great location. However, another church beat us to it. Our hopes were dashed, but we didn't give up.

Then we located three other pieces of land, but none of these seemed like the place. Next, we found another pre-existing building that seemed like a good fit, but it didn't work out either.

Then, we found a prime piece of real estate on a major highway with an already existing building. We just knew this was it. The only problem was the sellers wanted fifteen million dollars. But, we had a big faith in a big God so we weren't daunted.

So, when the owners reduced their selling price to seven million dollars we decided this must be our building. We contacted Hobby Lobby and they gave us the green light. They were willing to purchase this building for us.

We had an appraisal done and Hobby Lobby made an offer to purchase the building and give it to us. For days we waited on pins and needles to find out if the seller accepted the offer.

It was a sad day when my husband received a message telling us that the seller declined the offer. I remember standing in our living room looking at each other trying to figure out what to say. "God must be protecting us from something," Joe finally spoke up. "All we can do is trust Him through this. He must have something better."

My lips feigned agreement, but my heart was crushed. How could this happen? I just knew this was our land and building. Our church trusted us. They believed with us. Now what would we do?

As I write this book we still don't know what we are going to do. We are still waiting on God. We are still renting a building. We are still pressing through our disappointment. But more importantly, we are still expecting God to answer our prayers. We still have faith. We still believe. We still abide.

This story is our story of learning to abide. It's our story of learning to hold on to faith when the winds of doubt and delay threaten to blow it away.

All of us have a similar story; a story that involves delays and detours on our journey to abiding with God and holding on to His promises, a story that involves waiting and wondering why God didn't answer our prayers the way we expected, a story with an inexhaustible supply of reasons to doubt God's faithfulness, a story that has the potential to rob us of our hope and our dwelling place in God. It's a story that tries our faith and tests our endurance. It's a story that asks us to make choices. Because here's the thing: we get to choose how our story ends.

We get to choose if we give up and lose hope. We get to choose if we live in disappointment and hopelessness. We also get to choose if we will live in expectation and hope. We get to choose if we expect God to answer our prayers. We get to choose if we will press in to His presence. We get to choose to press out the demons of doubt. We get to choose to press on to greater levels of abiding. We get to choose to have faith in God. We get to choose to endure and to never give up. We get to choose.

I for one choose to press in, press out and press on. I hope you will too. We've come too far to give up now.

The other day my husband and I were watching a movie. I was so exhausted that I had to fight going to sleep for two whole hours. It wasn't that the movie wasn't good. It was a great movie and I wanted so badly to see how it ended. I was just so tired that I could hardly stay awake. However, despite my best efforts, I fell asleep the last ten minutes of the movie.

Sometimes life can be like watching a movie. We're so exhausted from fighting the battles that we fall asleep in the final scene. We grow so weary that we miss the ending. We miss out on the good things that God has in store for us. We fall asleep or fall away or fall down or fall short of our reward.

But, it doesn't have to be that way. We don't have to miss out on the good things that God has in store for us. Yes, we might grow weary. Yes, we might be discouraged. Yes, we might feel like giving up. But if we will wait on God we will have our reward. Habakkuk 2:3 says it like this:

For the vision is yet for the appointed time. It hastens toward the goal and it will not fail. Though it tarries, wait for it. For it will certainly come, it will not delay.

My husband and I have been waiting for our land and building for over a decade. Maybe you have been waiting for something as long or longer. I want to encourage you to hang in there and not give up.

James 1:2-5 tells us that the testing of our faith develops patience. Could it be that the delays in our life are God ordained? Could God be teaching us to be patient? James goes on to say that when we have patience, we are mature and complete, lacking nothing.

It's interesting to note that the biblical word for "patience" comes from the Greek word "hupomeno." It's a compound word that is derived from two words: hupo and meno. The word hupo means "under" – like to be underneath something. We already know that meno means "to stay or abide." How about that? We're right back where we started: learning to abide. In this definition you could say abide means to stay in one place, to keep a position, or to maintain whatever ground you've taken. It's similar to a soldier that has taken enemy territory and refuses to retreat. He will stand his ground and maintain his position no matter what the enemy says or does.

If we put these two words together we see that to be patient means to stay under whatever pressure comes against us without losing the ground we've gained. It's about persevering to the end. It's about holding out, holding on and holding up until we see the final outcome. It's about enduring and staying true to the promise and vision that God gave us. We're steadfast and unwavering until the end.

I conclude this book with this challenge: never give up! Stay your ground. Continue to abide in the presence of God. Let God dwell with you. Live your life in Christ. Cling to the expectation of living in God's presence and reaping the benefits of doing so. Let patience have her perfect work in you. If you're waiting for God to answer your prayers, keep waiting; never give up, no matter how long it takes. Abide in faith and expectation that God will answer. Press in, press out, and press on to live in God's presence.

Abiding in Christ is the only life worth living!

ABOUT THE AUTHOR

Deborah Oakley is a gifted communicator and speaker with a message that empowers others to discover their God-given destiny. Deborah has been in ministry for 30 years. She and her husband Joe have pastored two churches. In 2001, they established Grace Fellowship Church in Grand Prairie, Texas, a ministry committed to the vision of "Touching Heaven, Changing Earth." As Associate Senior Pastor of Grace Fellowship, Deborah's ministry includes preaching, teaching, writing, counseling, and mentoring leaders.

Deborah has her bachelor's degree in Theology from Christian International University. She and Joe have been married for 40 years and have 2 children and 6 grandchildren.

Deborah also travels and speaks at women's and leadership conferences and preaches powerful anointed messages. To listen to her messages, or more for information on Grace Fellowship Church, visit their website at www.gfc.cc

Abide

Made in the
USA
Middletown, DE